People Are Saying . . .

This book is absolutely fabulous. Anyone in direct sales who uses social media for business should read this book. It will help you immensely with building your business, as well as keeping your friends from un-following you. It helps you avoid some major social or legal blunders. The book is easy to read and right off the bat, after just a paragraph you'll learn useful things to help you in your business.

Mary Bacon
Senior Group Leader with Steeped Tea
mysteepedteaparty.com/marybacon

*I love the common sense and quick to apply ideas. The list of post ideas make business promotion on Facebook elegant and a no-brainer to implement. All of the ways you suggest to gently open up a discussion on business are just fantastic and **will open up opportunities** when consistently put into play.*

Traci Brown
Body Language and Persuasion Expert
bodylanguagetrainer.com

*I can't recommend Karen Clark enough! I was so blessed to have her on our team at Women Speakers Association. She is impeccable at what she does! If you're in direct sales...Heck! Even if you're not in direct sales but you're looking to **use social media in an ethical and effective way** to connect with people, not collect people...you want to get Karen's book TODAY!*

Liora Mendeloff
Founder, Women Speakers Association
womenspeakersassociation.com

There's so much "noise" in social media with constant direct selling messages. Karen's book helps me differentiate my business from all the "Buy this from me!!!" messages. Connecting with people rather than collecting people as a means to an end – that's Karen's heart and mine too. Great book!

Denise Hensarling
Independent Mary & Martha Senior Team Leader
www.luke1042.com

This book should be on the **must-read list of all new, and seasoned direct sales representatives.** The Facebook section addressing not liking other consultants' pages from within your own company can be compared to cross-lining, also a no-no. Karen offers sound advice based on personal experience; the statements from other direct sales reps validates the information. As a nurse, I related to the comments on **CPR and 9-1-1 – they make perfect sense.**

Sharon M. Weinstein
Certified Speaking Professional, Author of *B is for Balance*
sharonmweinstein.com

To all my direct sales power women, Karen Clark knows her stuff regarding social media for direct selling. Her book is providing **real tools and content!**

Pegine Echevarria
Speaker and Author of
Sometimes You Need to Kick Your Own Butt
pegine.com

I have been in direct sales over ten years and have read many networking books! This book hits everything you need to know on social media. Thank you Karen! I can't wait to meet you in person!

Sarah Hipple
Independent Tyra Beautytainer
tyra.com/befiercelyfab

Social Media for Direct Selling Representatives is a must if you're working in the direct selling market. In just a few short lines author Karen Clark shares how you can **quickly increase your network** with a few simple steps. Books like these are mostly smoke and mirrors. Clark has lived and worked in the direct selling industry and knows what it takes to build a business from the ground up ~ the success of the tools and tips provided depends largely on you creating your conviction for success. Karen Clark rises to this challenge and **knocks it out of the park** with great skill in this accomplished and thoughtful book. A+++++

Connie Pheiff
President CPS, Inc.,
Business Growth Speaker, C-Suite Radio Host
conniepheiffspeaks.com

I wish I had read this book YEARS AGO! Karen Clark elevates the relationship-building skills you already have, showing you how to MERGE these with technology. As a former top performing direct sales leader, I KNOW this training will help you book, sell and sponsor more using the latest techniques, provided in an easy-to-follow manner. This book is a practical resource guide for anyone in the sales field who wants to ACCELERATE their business without losing the human touch.

Elizabeth McCormick
Motivational Speaker & Former Black Hawk Pilot
yourinspirationalspeaker.com

How refreshing and wonderful that someone has created a **comprehensive, creative, and well-crafted guide** for attracting and serving customers intentionally, ethically and effectively via social media!

Patti DeNucci
Author of *The Intentional Networker*
intentionalnetworker.com

As a creative director and graphic designer in the direct sales industry, Karen Clark has always been a wonderful resource for me and my business. Social media is a large part of my brand and the work that I provide for my clients. **Social Media For Direct Selling** is a must-have guide to navigate online marketing in today's world. Filled with **helpful knowledge, tips and tricks,** it's my new go-to guide that I can use practically every day!

Jess Gallant

Art Direction, Design & Marketing for Direct Sales

jessgallant.com

I devoured your **Social Media for Direct Selling Representatives** book on the airplane today. It is chock full of **practical, helpful advice** that ANYONE in a sales-centric position can use right away. I particularly resonated with your CPR and 9-1-1 strategies, as I have found myself getting overwhelmed with what to do on social media. They were just what I needed to **clear away all of the noise** and focus me on what I can and WILL do every single day to grow my business! Every single person who sells to another should get your book! I'm already sharing it.

Theresa Rose

Sales, Marketing & Leadership Expert

Award-Winning Author

theresarose.com

This book is long overdue. In the ever-changing landscape of social media, sound education for the field representative has failed to trickle down in many cases. Representatives are left to "figure it out" as they go. This book offers a bevy of information from defining your social media brand to postings to understanding the metrics. What I love most about Karen's style is that **she never lets you forget people are at the heart of social media.** I would recommend this book at the top of the list for every direct seller. No matter how well-versed you are, you are sure to learn a few new tricks and your results will be all the better for it.

Michelle Archer
Founder and CEO at Direct Sales Institute
directsalesinstitute.com

What an amazing resource. This is a powerhouse engine and guide for your direct selling business! I've spoken, emceed and performed for many direct sales groups through the years and been a direct seller myself for different companies. I'm also very conscientious about staying on top of the latest social media best practices and trends and without a doubt know how **social media is the lifeblood now for direct sellers**. Karen's book is a priceless hand-holding step by step asset that will help you cut through all the noise that can overwhelm you out there, giving you a **clear path of exactly what you need to do (and NOT do).** Brilliantly written and invaluable resource. Thanks Karen!

Lynn Rose
High Performance Expert, Dynamic Keynoter &
Energizing Entertainer: *The POWER To WOW*
lynnrose.com

SOCIAL MEDIA
FOR DIRECT SELLING
Representatives

SOCIAL MEDIA
FOR DIRECT SELLING
Representatives

KAREN CLARK

Connections Press
Rohnert Park, California

Connections Press
PO Box 1264
Rohnert Park, CA 94927

Publishing Website: connectionspress.com

Book Website: socialmediafordirectselling.com

General Website: mybusinesspresence.com
Email: karen@mybusinesspresence.com

Phone: 707-939-5709

Cover design by Angie Alaya, Pro eBook Covers
Cover illustration ©Vasilev_Ki/depositphotos.com
Author headshot by Scott R. Kline, srkheadshotday.com

Book midwife, final edit, interior layout design:
Ruth Schwartz, thewonderlady.com

Ordering Information:
Special discounts are available on quantity purchases by corporations, associations and others. For details, contact the "Special Sales Department" at the above address.

Social Media for Direct Selling Representatives / Karen Clark — 1st ed.
ISBN: 978-0-9971016-0-7
Library of Congress Control Number: 2015920323

*For Greg, who supports my dreams and
for Fallon, Alia and Terry, who inspire me!*

Acknowledgements

Having been a contributing author to five previous books with amazing co-authors, writing my own book at last has been quite a thrill! I have been a content marketer since 1998, and was an English grammar and composition major in college. Writing comes easily to me, but for some reason it took this long to develop and publish my own book. With a few nudges from people who saw this missing piece before I did, I was able to visualize not just this book, but a series of multiple publications that enable me to share my knowledge. I have many people — friends, family and colleagues — to thank for their roles in this journey, and only some of them are highlighted here.

First and foremost is the love, patience and support of my family. As I have been building my career as a business consultant and speaker, they have never hesitated to step up and pitch in, or keep things running at home while I travel. Greg, you are the rock that gives me the freedom to fly, and the laughter that puts a spring in my step. Fallon, Alia and Terry, your curiosity and enthusiasm inspire me, and your pursuit of your goals is unshakable. Mothering you will always be my greatest source of pride. My parents, George and Sandi, and my in-laws, Terry and Aletta, have been incredibly supportive throughout my journey, despite not always understanding why

I do what I do. I know without a doubt I would not have been able to work from home, travel for speaking engagements, and still truly be there for the kids without them.

My cousin and best friend, Cheryl Sandberg, was my original "partner in crime" with regard to learning how to code websites and blogs, work Photoshop, and connect with people online. Her technical expertise, people skills and support as a business partner throughout the years, beginning with helping develop my first website when I was in the field, has been invaluable.

I'd also like to thank the organizers and speakers involved with the Direct Selling Edge conferences whose expertise, feedback and advice played an integral role in helping me bridge the gap between the needs of field representatives and corporate objectives. Jay Leisner, Kevin Thompson, Victoria Dohr, Troy Dooly, and Donna Marie Serritella — thank you.

When I first started my direct sales journey, and began to transition as a professional speaker, three organizations played key roles in helping me find my own voice as a trainer. The Direct Selling World Alliance (formerly known as the Direct Selling Women's Alliance) provided the first platform on which I was able to teach Internet marketing to an audience from companies I was not directly involved in. As one of the first ELITE Leadership® Certification Program graduates, the DSWA's core values of service, trust, authenticity, integrity and respect have stayed with me and are reflected in my trainings.

The team at Productive Learning, a personal development organization, has empowered me over the years to become more aware of the unconscious thoughts and assumptions that have held me back in business as well as in the rest of my life. Through their guidance and interactive workshops, I have gained clarity about who I am, what I am truly capable of and the extraordinary future in front of me.

Finally, when I discovered the National Speakers Association, whose Code of Ethics recognizes the characteristics of honesty, leadership and stewardship, I knew I had found a home in the business world. The support and encouragement of its members has inspired me to move forward on my dreams without compromising my values.

I'd like to also acknowledge Jennifer Harmon, direct sales training specialist, who was instrumental in providing feedback while collaborating with me on my online party training. She helped me innovate and stretch, while also making sure the training I provide independent consultants is in alignment with the needs of the direct selling companies that they represent.

To Ruth Schwartz, my Book Midwife—also known as The Wonderlady—I cannot thank you enough for allowing me to tap into your book publishing expertise to finally, finally produce this work for all to see. Without your encouragement and patience, this would still be "something I think I will do someday" instead of something those who need what I know can use today. Your professionalism, creativity and eagle eye are appreciated!

And last, I'd like to thank the many direct selling companies and representatives who entrusted me over the years to help them navigate the ever-changing world of online marketing. Your belief in me and my expertise, even when it was scary and unfamiliar, humbles me. Your appreciation of information that is both easy to understand and implement—yet also professional and results-producing—will remain at the forefront as I continue to develop my publications and trainings. Thank you for braving the digital world with me!

Table of Contents

Introduction 1

How to Use This Book.. 7

Bonus Resources.. 11

Social Media Best Practices

Words to the Wise.. 15

Social Media Sites Explained.................................... 19

A Bit More About Facebook....................................... 29

Social Media CPR... 35

What to Post? Follow the 9-1-1 Code 41

Finding Your Social Media Voice 47

Your Business Values 53

Social Media Post Ideas.. 57

Measuring Social Media's ROI (Return on Interaction) ... 67

Scheduling and Automation 71

Organic Social Media.. 75

Customer Service Through Social Media 79

People Before Things... 83

Avoid Common Problems

Don't Be Boring 89

Avoid Negative Comments.. 93

How to Avoid "Facebook Jail"................................... 97

Do Not Like Each Others' Facebook Pages 105

Avoiding Litigation When Posting Images 111

Sharing the Business Opportunity 115

Social Media Do's and Don'ts 121

Social Media Parties

Social Media Parties Pros & Cons 133

Host Coaching for Social Media Parties 141

New Guidelines for Facebook Parties 147

Facebook Parties How-To 153

Questions About Facebook Parties 173

Instagram Parties How-To 181

Pinterest Parties How-To 191

Additional Online Marketing

Run a Facebook Contest! 201

Promote Your Business in Online Directories 207

Submit Your Product to Product Review Blogs 211

Serving the Mom & Grandma Market Online 215

In Closing . . .

Final Thoughts 223

Contributors 227

Connect with Karen Clark 234

Use This Book as a Training Tool 235

Introduction

I'm Karen Clark and I'm here to teach you that the **high tech** world of social media and Internet marketing is—and should be—a **high touch** world full of relationships. I am talking about meaningful mutual relationships, since it's really about *connecting* with people, not *collecting* people!

My Story

When I first started in direct selling I was living in Florida in a troubled marriage. As a military mom I felt alone and isolated, and when my opportunity came along, I grabbed it with all my heart. Direct selling was a way—frankly—to distract myself from what was going on at home, yet also still be there for my two young children. I was excited to be meeting new people every day, inspiring and educating them about my business. I didn't even know it, but I was looking for a connection to others, and also a sense of belonging and a home where I'd feel supported and appreciated. I found that in direct selling.

Six weeks after joining, the rug was pulled out from under me. Just as I hit my "Quick Start" qualification we found out we were being transferred from northwest Florida all the way to Washington state. I didn't know what to do regarding my business. One day I was rocking and rolling, sometimes doing three parties a week—even bringing my daughters with me most of the time. I was really loving the business! The next day I was devastated to hear it was time again to move. What would happen to my Florida customers? How could I start over in Washington—a place where I knew no one—not a soul? How would I replace the income we had begun to count on without having to go back to teaching school?

I looked to the Internet and even though the web was still fairly young—this was 1998, which is like centuries ago in Internet years—what I found there were the very early beginnings of social media. I found communities of moms, communities of military wives and communities of wives of alcoholics. I found teacher forums, recipe swaps, and email groups for nursing mothers. I found CONNECTION.

What's even more exciting is I found team members for my direct selling business. I found customers and I found hosts. I started teams in states where the company had never been, where no one had ever even heard of us. What I found online was that there were people just like me looking for connections, support, and a source of income so that they too could contribute to their family or stay home with their kids, meet people, or even escape a bad situation.

I also began building a team in my new state of Washington because I was able to meet them online before I even got there! I built relationships in advance, found out about vendor fairs for the holiday period, set up an open house, and began to book home parties. When we arrived in Washington, I was already in business there and my personal volume and team building did not skip a beat. I had discovered the power of Internet marketing.

I quickly advanced through the ranks of our company and was brought on to develop training programs and work with leaders directly throughout the entire company. Over the twelve years I was with that company I grew leaders and teams all over the United States, some of whom are still the best friends I've ever had. The Internet is an amazing web of people and if you do it the way I've done it, you'll find yourself successful and fulfilled beyond your wildest dreams.

It's Time for a Shift

Fast forward to today and I have to say, I've got a new life now, including a new man, and a third child. I've left my position within that company and since 2010 I've been on a new mission!

Now I am looking for a SHIFT in the direct selling profession — a shift from blatantly broadcasting messages like 'buy my stuff' 'join my team' and 'book a party' over and over — to truly connecting and building relationships online. My goal is that direct selling becomes associated with people of service and integrity. We can do that through social media.

We are the original social network! It took us a long time to get direct selling companies into the Internet. We are a "people to people" profession and corporate executives were cautious and concerned about losing that connection. But now that social media is very mainstream, companies have embraced it as a way to allow their representatives to advocate for their businesses across the country, and in some cases, all over the world. However, now we are finding that the pendulum has swung the other way and sometimes direct sellers are overdoing it! It's time to find a balance.

I get it — you are excited about your opportunity or your product and how it can change lives. If you are anything like I was while I was in the field, your business is your LIFE. It's where your friends are, your family, your work time and your leisure time, your vacation and your income. You are living, eating, and breathing your business! But that doesn't mean the rest of the world wants to hear about it several times a day every day on social media.

So I decided to write this book to teach you, direct sellers who truly love to connect with people, how best to use social media. When you are online, marketing your business, everything you post is a reflection of who you are as a business person, what your company stands for, and it's a reflection of the entire profession. We have an opportunity to reach hundreds of thousands of people, so it's important to put your best self out there, starting with a professional online presence!

But there are challenges: too many tools, how to get results with them, how to use them, and how to do it in less time so we can get back to the other demands on our time—home, family, self-care, and other obligations.

In this book I am going to explore ideas, strategies and tactics to help you take your business to the next level. No matter where you are with using social media— whether you picked this up because it's finally time to start, or whether you've been using social media for a while but would like to know how to get more out of it—you will benefit from this book. Depending on your level of experience with technology, some of this will make sense and some will need more explanation. One of the benefits of purchasing this book is that you will also have the opportunity to access a Resource Page so that you can take a deeper dive if you wish. I also encourage you to join my Karen on Call program, a private group where your questions are welcomed and additional training is offered.

You Have Questions, We Have Answers

Join my community of entrepreneurs who are navigating the world of social media. Learn answers to questions you have about building your business using technology, while learning from the questions that others have. In my Karen on Call program you will receive:

- Get a minimum of one live teleclass per month where you can ask questions of me.

- Learn the latest news in social media marketing, changes to platforms and best practices.

- Participate in a private discussion group where, any time you need it, you can safely troubleshoot any tech trouble you come across while marketing your business online.

- Get access to past training calls, videos, and bonus content.

It's like having your own "tech support" any time you need it. Find out more at ***KarenonCall.com*** and receive your first month free.

I would say that I was extremely technically challenged. Anything techie usually made my eyes cross and have me run from my computer. I really struggle in this area of my business and generally just hired people to do it for me, instead of learning something new. I started reading some of Karen's articles and listened to some of her training, and they were terrific! They spurred me on to learn more and instead of dreading technical things, I started seeking out new ways to do things, and read more articles and tips. I figured out that Instagram, Periscope, Twitter etc. are not hard to use once you know

how. Thanks Karen for putting the techie spark in me! Now I love it and can't wait to find the newest, latest and greatest to try out.

Terra Larsen

Independent Consultant, National Director, Epicure

facebook.com/terralarsen

How to Use This Book

Before you dive into the following chapters, I wanted to be sure we are all on the same page, so to speak, about a few things. This book was written with the independent direct selling representative in mind. Although some of the principles apply to general business entrepreneurs, the intended audience is made up of the individual business owners who represent a company in the direct selling industry. As such, there are a few distinctions you might notice.

About Direct Selling

Direct selling representatives are independent consultants, distributors or business owners who represent a direct selling company. There is some confusion about what constitutes direct selling, but for the purpose of this book and my readers, direct selling is the business model where a company allows independent contractors to sign an agreement to sell the company's products for a commission, working as an independent representative, sometimes directly to customers (one on one) and sometimes in a group demonstration or party environment. There is a multi-tiered pay plan that allows the representative to also get a percentage of the sales garnered by someone that they introduce the business to who also signs up, and any additional people who are enrolled by that person.

Within the business designation of "direct sales" there are two basic models: Party Plan and Network Marketing/MLM. Technically person-to-person sales, such as door-to-door selling, is also a direct selling or direct sales option, but is far less typical and operates very differently than what we are discussing in this book.

Party Plan representatives typically conduct the vast majority of their business by selling products through group gatherings known as home parties, shows, or gatherings, and by bringing others into the business. They may also choose to sell through online parties or virtual shows, which are also group situations. In these gatherings, there is often a separate person who acts as the host and invites his or her friends to attend the demonstration or sales talk. The host is then rewarded with free or discounted product in exchange for introducing the product to people she knows. Although Party Plan representatives also sell product in other settings—such as vendor fairs, craft shows, fundraisers, one on one appointments and more—the primary business model is selling to a group of individuals at one time. The emphasis with Party Plan companies is on product sales. Therefore there are often seasonal, annual or bi-annual new product introductions, monthly product specials, and monthly exclusive product for hosts.

Network Marketing/MLM representatives generally conduct most of their business through networking one on one, through word of mouth, and through referrals from the people they meet. Networking with other individuals is key, and doing so in person or by phone, online or other communication methods is most common, though some Network Marketing representatives also like to set up group demonstrations, tastings and informational events. Network Marketing representatives are paid commission on the sale of their products as well as enrolling both customers and business builders in the business. In the pay plans, there are typically a variety of incentives to bring on additional representatives, building a large team of people that will also begin enrolling others.

Who Was this Book Written For?

Much of this book is directed to both Party Plan and Network Marketing/MLM representatives and I welcome people from both business models to take the advice that appeals to them the most. Since my background is from being with a Party Plan company, and since I primarily work with Party Plan companies and their representatives, you might find that some of the chapters and some of the language leans more toward the Party Plan way of doing things. For example there are several chapters on conducting social media parties. These generally will appeal to those in Party Plan companies. However, they can be adapted to those in Network Marketing/MLM as well because they really are another version of networking and sharing information, regardless of the type of company you are with.

Since the vast majority of Party Plan representatives are female, I have decided to use the pronouns "she" and "her" throughout the book, even though I recognize that there are many male representatives as well. In fact, the average Network Marketing representative is male. Rather than alternate between male and female, I made the call to go with female for the purposes of this book.

Other labels you may see in this book would be the terms used for representatives. Companies vary in this and you may find I varied my terminology as well. Consultants or distributors are labels I typically use for representatives.

Stay in Compliance

Since you are more than likely a direct selling representative reading this book, I'd like to mention that the chapters were written in a general way to apply to anyone in direct sales. The advice is not company-specific and your own company may have guidelines that differ from mine. Staying in compliance with your company's policy is vital, so please keep that in mind. I work with many companies and have attempted to accommodate most, but there are some I'm unfamiliar with. I cannot take responsibility for you taking actions that may not be in alignment with your company. Always check with your Policies & Procedures or with the home office directly if you aren't sure whether something is allowed. It's up to you to cross check with your company, or even suggest policy changes if you find they could use some updating. This is not unheard of.

Connecting, Not Collecting

I invite you to use what you learn in this book to make a shift in how you see social media marketing — not only what it can do for you, but what you can do for others. With the ideas presented here, you can reach more people, truly serve and connect with people — not collect people — and grow your business one post at a time, one picture at a time, one day at a time and *still* have time for the rest of your life!

Bonus Resources

Social media platforms, best practices, and technology shift very rapidly, and sometimes without warning. If you've ever opened your Facebook to see things completely rearranged, you know what I am talking about! As you can imagine, writing a book about social media and Internet marketing is challenging for this reason. There is always a risk that by the time my readers receive their book, something will be out-of-date.

Social media is always evolving. To help keep up with changes that may occur, I've created a special Resource Page for anyone who has purchased this book. By registering for our private resource page, you have the opportunity to receive updates to any of the chapters as they may come up, as well as bonus material that will help you further implement what you learn in this book. I have purposely left the detailed how-to's of each social media platform out of this book, knowing that they change the fastest. You will find, however, PDFs of these on this Resource Page. I will update those periodically as well.

Register here to receive the link and password by email:
smdsbook.com/resources

Social Media Best Practices

Words to the Wise

Before we go further, here are some things to consider when using social media:

1. **Don't go nuts!** Your business is seeing, talking to, and being with people, demonstrating your products, conducting in-home or virtual parties, supporting your team—not being on social media all day. No matter how much you love online marketing, there needs to be a balance between your online and offline activities. Be mindful of the time you are spending.

2. Nothing online will ever, in my opinion, replace offline experiences in social settings, whether it's an in-home party, a vendor boutique or a coffee shop meeting. You simply cannot replicate the experience of seeing and touching your product, talking, sharing, smiling, laughing, and influencing others to take action. Try as we may, those just can't be duplicated online. There are ways you can come close, but it is never quite the same. **Using social media is a supplement.** It is one part of your overall marketing mix that helps you meet more people and stay in touch—and perhaps service long distance customers, hosts and team members—but

your business is so much more. Some of the best relation-ships start online but if someone is local to you, there's no reason why you can't turn it into an offline relationship, too!

3. **There are rules.** Be sure that you have read and understand both your company policies and procedures regarding so-cial media and Internet marketing, and each social media platform's Terms of Service. These are documents you agree to when you sign up. Read them. Just because you see someone else doing something that looks like a great idea, it does not mean it is permissible. It is your responsibility as a business owner to keep yourself informed and in compli-ance, protecting yourself from any repercussions.

4. **You are always modeling for others.** Everything that you do in your business, whether you want it to be or not, is po-tentially going to be duplicated by your team—or the future team you may not even be aware of yet. If you are making your phone calls, they will be making their phone calls. If you are doing home parties, they will be doing home par-ties. If you are sponsoring, they will be sponsoring. If you are on Facebook twelve hours a day, neglecting your other obligations, they will be on Facebook twelve hours a day doing the same! Make sure you are modeling online the be-haviors you want from your team or future team.

As a business consultant for direct selling companies, owners have commented to me that the field tends to do their own social media marketing without first reading their policies and procedures, which are put in place for their own protection and for the integrity of the company. Doing what you want to do regardless of the P&P can affect

the reputation of the entire company, representatives and owners. It is important for social media policies to be enforced by Corporate, but it starts with representatives taking responsibility for their own businesses by making sure they are in compliance. This benefits everyone.

Victoria Dohr,

Senior Consultant, Sylvina Consulting

twitter.com/sylvina

Social Media Sites Explained

Direct selling is a relationship business and in the online presence world, relationships are also key. I like to think of the Internet as parallel to a real life social party or networking event. Some people are friends, some are acquaintances and many in attendance are people you have not yet met. You have the potential of meeting new people who may or may not be interested in what you have to offer, and likewise they may have something you are interested in as well.

I do not believe the typical entrepreneur or small business owner should be actively—meaning daily—participating on anything and everything out there. Pick something that feels right and seems to work well for you as far as results, or where your ideal customer is hanging out. Maximize your presence there, although setting up basic profiles in the others makes sense in case people are there who want to find someone who does just what you do!

For example someone who is in direct selling might focus just on Facebook, and maybe have a LinkedIn profile they work on once a week for the business networking aspect, and maybe also do Pinterest or Instagram when they feel like it. However, those other platforms aren't the main driving force behind building their online presence. Someone who loves photography might decide that Instagram is their main focus and they do all they can to leverage hashtags and other tools to promote their business—along with Pinterest once in a while—and create albums on Facebook for prospects to see. A top leader might want to focus mainly on LinkedIn where they can use its search feature to network with people looking for work. They may also use a private Facebook group for coaching their team, to build community and offer ongoing training in addition to what the company provides. Pinterest and Instagram might not be as prominent for them but they may use them for personal reasons.

Many of the social media sites can be integrated to save you time and cross post. When I first started teaching social media marketing it was really frowned upon to post the same thing to several social media sites because your audience would be seeing repeats. I still believe that is true to some extent, but what I am also finding is that now that social media is more mainstream and pretty much everyone has at least one of the sites they use regularly, general users, that is non-business people, seem to have segmented themselves into just one or two sites. So today, chances are that Facebook people ONLY use Facebook, Twitter people ONLY use Twitter, and LinkedIn people ONLY use LinkedIn. They may check the others once in a while but they certainly are not going to see all your posts all the time repeated over and over. Because of that I do think it saves time and increases your exposure to cross-post when you have something useful and important and when it seems to fit more than one audience.

For example, I will sometimes post a personal picture that is related to my business—such as a travel picture—to my Instagram, but I will also click the box to let it post to my Facebook Business Page and Twitter at the same time. I may find something really awesome on Pinterest to share and save it to one of my Pinterest boards, but then also post it to Facebook and Twitter. Often when I write a blog post on my website, I will repost it onto my LinkedIn in the publishing area, and then tweet it out or share it on Facebook. This practice can help you build up more posts without having to reinvent the wheel every day, and also increase your exposure when the social media sites may not have shown your post to everyone. It gives you another chance to be seen!

I like to compare social media to a big party. What would you do or say, or how would you behave in a social situation offline if you wanted to attract people to your product or service? Would you go around shouting at them about how they should buy from you? Or would you get to know people, start conversations, share something about yourself? This is the kind of thinking I encourage you to start doing in your social media efforts, whether on your Personal Profiles or business accounts or pages.

Following is a list of the most popular social media sites where I compare them to a situation in "real life" and explain some basic differences. For specific how-to instructions for setting each of these up and how to use them, see the Resource Page *(smdsbook.com/resources)*.

Pinterest

To me, Pinterest is like that potluck party where everyone brings something to the table. As you look through the offerings you might decide to ask the person who brought it to share the recipe with you. You might write it down and put it in your folder of recipes you are going to try someday.

You might also think of Pinterest as a file cabinet of articles, recipes and crafts you're gong to do someday, or pictures from magazines of items you want to buy someday, that you've saved and organized by folders. Only this file cabinet and its folders are shared with your friends who can then save them to their own folders and file cabinets.

- Pinterest is a visual way of saving a website using an image that links to a site to find out more. The image saved onto the "board" or category is the visual reminder of what the article or website is about.

- What makes it great for business is that Pinterest is considered a shopping "discovery" site — people find things they love and BUY them.

- Because Pinterest is used primarily by women, the items shared there are mostly decorating ideas, entertaining and recipes, how-to's for crafts, and other homemaking related items, including gift ideas.

Ideas to Try:

1. When you share a post from the home office, click See Pin, then Edit, and then change the URL to your own link.

2. Start a board just about your business, in addition to related topics. Be sure to add a board description!

3. Start a Secret Board where you and your team can add related content. Then everyone can pin from it whenever they are ready to.

4. Start a Secret Team Support Board and share ideas for your business that they would like. Invite them to pin business-building tips on it, too.

Instagram

Have you ever gone to a friend's house and seen their photo albums out on a coffee table or on a shelf and been curious? Have you ever had someone visit your home for the first time and wander the halls looking at the photographs on your wall, or all over your refrigerator? Instagram is like that. It is a way to share mostly personal photographs with friends who look at them in order to get to know you better. They may give you their opinion, ask you a question, or otherwise remark on the photos that you share. In addition, when you post a photograph to Instagram there are many image editing options that allow you to filter colors and special effects into your photos to make them even more captivating.

For your business, Instagram gives people a window into your world, sharing those "Kodak moments" that allow people to get to know you both personally and professionally.

- Unless you are sponsoring a post, there are no clickable links to your website other than in your profile bio. Insta-gram is strictly for picture sharing, liking and commenting on the pictures people share.

- The use of descriptive #hashtags increases exposure to others who view pictures based on hashtags they are interested in. Try adding three to five relevant hashtags in the caption of your picture.

Ideas to Try:

1. Share incentive trip pictures, convention pictures, snapshots of displays, creative photos of people or objects

2. Add quirky captions and popular hashtags, which increase your exposure.

3. Click the Facebook or Twitter share buttons and share to either your Personal Profile or your Business Pages on Facebook and/or to your Twitter account as well.

4. Use apps such as Word Dream and Over to create fun quote pictures, but don't overdo the graphics. People love actual photographs on Instagram best.

LinkedIn

LinkedIn can be compared to a formal business networking meeting in your local community, such as a Chamber of Commerce or professional networking event. At those meetings, since everyone is coming to conduct business, gain referrals, or otherwise promote themselves, people generally dress more formally and work hard to put their best foot forward in order to demonstrate their expertise so that those in attendance will hire them or refer others to them. Because of this, the quality of the conversations tend to be at a higher level than other social media sites, and you are much less likely to see personal information or family-oriented posts.

- For direct sellers, it is your leadership ability as someone offering a home-based business opportunity that will matter. Consider positioning yourself as a leader that others would want to follow in order to attract new people to your team.

- Demonstrate, through your posts and comments, your expertise in conducting a home-based business.

Ideas to Try:

1. Pack your Personal Profile with rich keywords so that the people looking for what you do can find you, either through LinkedIn's search or through the traditional search engines.

2. Participate in networking discussion groups, asking your own questions or offering meaningful advice when appropriate.

3. Use the long-form "Publish a post" option to create blog-style posts about topics of interest to those you would like to attract. These articles are not for promoting your business, but to serve the readers. However, you are free to add a short bio or byline at the end, leading to your personal website.

Twitter

Twitter is the social media world's "happy hour" that takes place in a nightclub in the center of a metropolitan area's business district! It's loud, it's crowded, it's busy, and it's casual. Each person there has a voice and a message that they want to get heard, and it's your job to listen and participate in relevant conversations. Often this means going from group to group at this venue so that you don't miss anything. Sometimes, when you're at a busy club you pull someone aside to discuss a topic further, then move on to the next conversation and then the next. It's fast and furious but when you learn how to "work the room" the payoff can be great.

- Twitter is full of fast moving news broadcasts in short blasts of 140 characters each. Get to the point quickly, or direct people to where they can find out more on your website, blog or other social media site.

- Relationships on Twitter tend to be a little shallower. Twitter tends to be more about sharing articles on blogs or news items. When you do get into a conversation with someone about their content though, it can be a meaningful way to connect in a more casual way. Consider reaching out to those who post by replying with your own thoughts.

- Bloggers and younger people/college students use Twitter more often than other demographic groups, and they are great prospects for joining your company. Use the Twitter search to find people to follow and interact in a helpful way to attract them.

Ideas to Try:

1. Join in or conduct a "tweet chat" or "twitter party." This is where everyone at a set time uses the same hashtag phrase, allowing you to follow conversations about a specific topic. Try #gno which stands for Girls Night Out. On Tuesday evenings a group of mom bloggers meets and discusses parenting topics. Participating exposes you to their members, and it is a lot of fun, too!

2. Twitter is increasingly being used as a login tool or connected account for other social media sites and tools such as live video streaming. Because of this, users are able to continue conversations on Twitter that start elsewhere. Even if you are not using Twitter on a daily basis, always check in to see if there are replies or private messages to attend to.

3. I do not recommend you use some of the tools available to "auto-DM" which means to automatically send a direct message to new followers. This can come across as inauthentic and needy. Instead, to greet new followers, do some research and strike up a real conversation about something

they are interested in, or ask them a question related to one of their more recent tweets.

Facebook

Facebook is the informal backyard barbecue of the social media world. It is casual, informal, fun and friendly. In general, people are mostly connected to friends and family they are close to off-line, with a mix of business contacts as well. At this barbecue, because of this mix, you'll want to make sure you are aware of the fact that you are always a reflection of your business (and your company, and the industry) so although it is informal, you might want to dress up a little bit (put your best jeans on) and then be prepared with business cards just in case! Even though the primary purpose for this barbecue is to connect with friends and family, when it's appropriate you certainly can talk about your business. It just isn't going to be your main focus. It's really the place you go to stay connected to anything you care about.

- Facebook users check Facebook daily, often before getting out of bed!

- The fastest growing segment on Facebook today is among women over 50 years old.

- If allowed, create a Business Page for your direct selling business and use it within your company guidelines. Personal Profiles are not intended to be used for commercial purposes, so be careful to only share business-related items occasionally on your main Facebook Profile and use your Business Page for more direct marketing.

Ideas to Try:

1. Consider making your business contact information listed on your Personal Profile visible to the public, whether or not people are friends with you. This makes it easy for people you meet throughout Facebook to contact you without having to "friend" you.

2. If you do create a Business Page, make sure you list it as your most recent "work" in your Personal Profile About section. Facebook will create a clickable link over to your Business Page that curious people can explore. I do not recommend linking your work to your company's Facebook page as that might confuse your friends and social media contacts.

3. When commenting or liking other posts made by other businesses that serve a similar demographic to you, comment or like as your Business Page instead of your Personal Profile. This exposes you to the other businesses' networks.

As a leader it's important to try to keep up to date with social media. Although you may not prefer to use the different platforms, you want to be aware of them and survey your team on what they like to use and how they would like to connect with you. Connecting them with experts like Karen is an easy way to serve your team without having to be an expert at social media yourself.

Donna Sickinger,

Independent National Executive Director,

Pampered Chef Canada

facebook.com/pamperedchefdonnasickinger

A Bit More About Facebook

There are four main areas on Facebook so I want to go into a little more detail here.

Personal Profile

This is like your home.

- Usually your connections here will be friends and family, and sometimes your team, but it is not intended to be used primarily for business. Doing so is against Facebook rules.

- Your business is integrated into your LIFE so what you do will be what you talk about—just be subtle and conversational.

- Be aware of any post in your News Feed that has a globe/public icon. These posts are public and any interaction you have with them—liking, commenting or sharing—generates a "story" that goes out to your whole network. This is great when the content is something that would appeal to the masses. But if you want to make a political rant on a local news story, be aware that if the post is public, all your Facebook friends will see what you commented and be able to read all the posts. I always check the privacy level of posts I interact with.

- Be sure to have your business information in your About section including a full description, maybe your "why" story, a list of products or categories, etc. Even though this is your Personal Profile, it is okay to include business information on your About section.

- Use your Personal Profile to build your network and give people a chance to get to know you. As your network expands, transition to using a Business Page.

- Be sure to include your website link and maybe links to your other social media sites.

- If someone requests you as a Facebook friend and you would rather keep them off your Personal Profile, simply private message them letting them know you are limiting your Personal Profile friends but would love to connect on your Business Page, and then give them the link.

- In your Facebook Account Settings find the Followers setting on the left and be sure to turn that function on to be visible to Everybody. That way even non-Friends can see posts you mark Public, such as things about your business.

Business Page

This is like your shop.

- Either brand yourself (Karen's Pleasant Products) or use your real name and independent consultant as the title. This is only allowable on Business Pages, not Personal Profiles. Check your company policy for page name guidelines, too.

- Pages are indexed by the search engines, so use good keywords within your descriptions and posts that people might be searching for.

- Be sure to include locations that you serve when filling out your About page—such as "Serving the areas of X, Y and Z, including the communities of A, B, C, and D." This way, when someone is looking on the search engines for a representative in those cities, your Facebook page will come up!

- Leverage your home office's posts when you want to promote something. No need to reinvent the wheel. Simply share the post to your page and add your own caption, and perhaps your link, so it brings the business to you.

- Do not like other consultants' pages from within your company. This hurts everyone's reach, because Facebook's algorithm is looking for people who like the page and also interact with it, and your fellow consultants aren't likely to do that. If you want to keep up with them, add them to an Interest List instead.

- Pages are very customizable. There are even services to create free application tabs you can add to your page such as an Instagram or Pinterest tab.

- Check your Insights to see which posts get the most reach or engagement—and do more like those!

- Use the Suggest Page feature (on the drop-down menu at the bottom right of your cover) to invite your email contacts to Like your page.

- If your company allows you to use paid advertising, consider using the Boost option for even $1 (scroll to Choose your own in the pricing area) to get additional exposure when you are posting something promotional. Boost the post to people who like your page.

Events

This is like your open house, or a party.

- Events can be created through your Personal Profile, a Business Page or a Facebook Group.

- Use Facebook events with care. Do not abuse them by creating them for non-events just to get some visibility.

- Events are best used as a supplement to a live in-person home party or other offline event. They are great for gathering RSVPs, conducting conversations around the party event (before and after) and for reminding people to attend. They can really help increase attendance when used correctly.

- Use a Facebook event as a way to follow up with RSVPs after separate personal invitations have been made—not as a replacement for personal invitations.

- Do not invite people who you haven't gotten a Yes or a Maybe from offline, or who do not want to be added, because they may begin receiving notifications and may mark the event as spam.

- Use Facebook events as an invitation to Opportunity Calls to help increase attendance.

- Consider setting up a form at Google Forms and pasting the link to the form in the event, and doing a drawing that awards a random person a door prize. Use the contacts you collected to follow up after your event

- When conducting sales, Facebook recommends using a Business Page, not your Personal Profile or a group. See more about this in our Social Media Parties chapter on page 135.

Groups

This is like your club or perhaps your reference desk.

- If you are a leader, Facebook groups are great for building community through conversations and really achieving a sense of connection with your team.

- Join your company's group for Consultants or Leaders if they provide one, in addition to whatever you set up yourself. Or if your upline leader has a support group, participate in that.

- Use the Files area to upload any PDFs, images or documents to share with your team or other members.

- You can also create a group for VIP customers or hosts and give them the inside scoop first, or allow them to ask questions and share how they are using your product.

- If you are conducting your own team group or customer group, consider a discussion question of the week, or a different topic every day such as Motivational Monday, Tip Tuesday, etc.

Now that we understand the basic idea of each of the social media sites, the next few chapters will explain more about what to post and how to behave when using each of them to market your direct selling business.

Facebook has been effective for me in following up with friends and communicating with my clients. We have established closed Facebook groups so that people who decide to do our amazing nutritional programs belong to a supportive community. Here we can share our wins, our questions, our tips, and motivation. We also share events and announcements. I love introducing the new people on our team. They are excited and feel supported.

Another way I've been using Facebook is communicating with our growing global team. We use the group to recognize accomplishments, root for team members, and post valuable training and resources. We are all blessed that Facebook and social media in general has made the whole world seem so close together. The sky is the limit as far as growing a global business using social media.

Imee Birkett,
Isagenix Health & Wealth
facebook.com/imeebirkett

Social Media CPR

Now that you understand the basic concepts of each social media site you might be asking yourself how you will manage your time so that you can be active on social media when you already have other important business tasks to handle, along with family and perhaps work obligations.

Social Media CPR is a formula I developed that allows you to manage your time on social media in about 15 to 20 minutes per day. You do not need to perform CPR on a daily basis on each of the platforms, but I recommend that you choose your favorite and do this consistently on at least that one platform in order to get the best results.

For Facebook this might look like one to three times per day, for LinkedIn, maybe one to three times per week, and for Twitter, five or more times per day. Other social media sites can be even less frequent if you like but if you use Social Media CPR when you do participate in them, you will be more effective. At the very least, when starting out with CPR, make a point to go into your social media sites and check for any replies or comments that you might need to attend to. Here's how it works:

C = COMMENT

Find three to five posts that other people or pages have made within your news feeds, and leave a meaningful comment. On Facebook, this can be either as your Personal Profile, or as your Business Page (on other Pages). For LinkedIn you might comment on items in the status updates, or discussions in Groups you may belong to, or on published posts. For Twitter, you would comment as a reply, mention or retweet of items that come through the main news feed, or items you find through searching. Instagram and Pinterest both have Like and Comment functions as well.

The idea is to renew awareness about you or your business among your connections, and to be interactive and social, not "sales-y." Your comments should add something to the conversation whenever possible, so that you can begin to build additional connections.

Simply find three to five items of interest in the main news feed that you can comment on in a way that adds to the conversation. If the people you comment toward are your ideal prospects or in your target demographic, even better.

Ideas to Try:

- Make it easier to comment on the right people's posts by sorting your contacts first. On LinkedIn it's called "tags" and on Facebook and Twitter you have Lists or Friend Lists where you can categorize people. Spend most of your CPR time interacting with people you want to build relationships with.

- Comment within Groups you belong to.

- Make sure you are posting comments that are useful and add to the conversation. Don't ever share your business information in a comment unless asked to.

P = POST

The key to posting on social media sites is consistency. With consistency your Profile or Page will build up momentum, which aids in it being found in the news feeds and search engines. Post at least once a day to both Personal Profile (if using one) and Business Page on Facebook. This is important to gain visibility in the news feed as Facebook rewards consistent posting. Post status updates, published articles or group discussions on LinkedIn, and three to ten tweets on Twitter. Post a photo a few times a week on Instagram and for Pinterest I tend to post three to five items all on the same day. Again for most direct sellers you will not need to be doing all of these—pick your favorite.

On all the platforms, your posts can consist of original text that you write, quotations or excerpts of others, photos or images you create, links to other articles, or links to videos. Using the share button functionality is useful as well.

When you are out on the web and come across a website or blog post your readers may be interested in, look for the social media share buttons as well. These allow you to easily post to your social media profiles and share interesting and relevant information with your audience. Try using a service such as *Buffer.com* to "queue" these share-posts up for later. If you begin to feel like you are hitting a "writer's block" and running out of ideas of what to post in order to be consistent, browse through the ideas in my chapter about Social Media Post Ideas (page 59) and maybe one of the suggestions there will appeal to you or your readers.

Ideas to Try

- The right times of day to post really varies person to person. Try testing your own posts, and then use your page insights for clues as to what works best. Or simply post when it's most convenient for you to do so.

- Be sure to switch up the types of post you make, such as text only, links, images, videos, and shares from other Business Pages.

- If really necessary, use appropriate social media scheduling tools such as the built in Schedule button on Facebook. See my chapter on Scheduling and Automation on page 73 to learn more.

R = REPLY

At the end of the work day, the next morning, or when you have a chance throughout the day after you have posted something, check your social media sites for any comments you have received on items that you posted. The idea is that when someone speaks to you, you would acknowledge him or her and respond — just like in your offline "real life."

This is an opportunity to stand out in social media because many of the larger brands do not interact, so their readers and fans never know if they or their comments have been seen.

You do not need to reply to every single comment, but at the end of the day if you respond back in general, those who commented will see that you have checked in, and know that you are hands-on. They will then get the idea that, if they interact on your page, you will respond. This is very valuable! Your response can even spark more conversation on that post which helps keep your community engaged and increases your visibility. Make it your goal to always be the last one to respond in a "thread" of comments on your social media posts.

Ideas to Try:

- Watch for "green flags" that indicate someone is interested in further information and take it offline ASAP to build the relationship through private messaging or chat. Don't push — be conversational and curious!

- Check your inbox/private messages regularly. On Facebook be sure to check your Business Page inbox as well. Often a prospect will not be as comfortable asking for more information publicly, but will message you privately.

Social Media CPR is easy to remember to do every day. Comment, Post, Reply. Doing these three things on a regular and consistent basis will help you reach more new people, build trust among those to whom you are already connected, and get you more results — all in less time.

I've learned to keep posting on Facebook — people are watching even if they don't comment. Most people who say they are not interested or who are silent will often contact me months down the road when they have a need that I can fill. I keep posting my amazing results and how my products have changed our lives. I don't pressure people. I put the information out there and let them come to me! I feel blessed to partner with such an amazing company. Once customers try our products, they always come back and that makes for happy customers!

Rhoda Kindred,

SRKINDRED — Independent Shaklee Distributor

facebook.com/srkindred

Basically social media is so much fun but once you connect there for me it's about taking it to the next level .... in person! So whenever I schedule a meeting in person what I do is dress professionally and then for a twist I put my business nametag on upside down. When I arrive early at let's say a coffee shop, the first thing I do is get in line and almost within seconds some one notices the name badge and kindly will tell me it's upside down.

I usually say, "Oh yeah! Wow... Well at least I will be able to read it and remember who I am and what I do. But seriously..." I say, "I was asked by my upline to make contact with five people who want to receive free product. Are you one of them? I have a drawing slip and you have a one in five chance of winning."

Usually about the time they are completing the form, my original appointment shows up and I share this technique with them to be able to make contact with others outside of social media while waiting to connect with someone from social media.

Tammy Forsythe,

Tupperware — with a smile.

facebook.com/thinkoutsidethebowl

What to Post? Follow the 9-1-1 Code

When considering what to post in social media, I recommend what I call the 9-1-1 Code. This means that about 90% of your posts are non-promotional in nature, and you are marketing something in 10% of your posts. That accounts for the 9 and the first 1. The other 1 in the 9-1-1 Code is a bonus personal or casual post—just for fun, or something where you allow people to get to know you. Together these eleven posts make up a winning combination that serves your readers, giving them content they look forward to seeing.

Ninety percent of what you post online should be non-marketing messages so that 10% of the time, when you do blatantly promote your business, your readers are much more likely to act on it by liking or commenting on your post, referring people to you by sharing it, and believing that what you are offering is of benefit to them and their friends. They feel compelled to respond in some way because with the other 90% your posts, you were able to build up trust and rapport with them by giving them something.

Give value. Give service. Give information. Give inspiration. That builds trust. And in this day and age, if someone does not trust you, you will be out of business. It is so easy for someone to click to another website or find another Consultant. But the truth is that when you have trust, you have a loyal following who will not only do business with you themselves, they will send business to you because of how you are showing up online. They want to do business with you because they know you have their best interests at heart.

Therefore, I strongly feel that 90% of what you post online should consist of information, inspiration, how-to's, questions, links to articles, photos, videos and so on that people can use whether or not they ever do business with you — no strings attached. I challenge you to try this approach for a period of one month and watch what happens. You'll see the amount of comments on your posts will go up. You'll start creating a culture that encourages conversations. You'll have the start of a loyal community built around your business, whichever platform you are using.

By the way, posting 90% non-marketing messages does not mean your readers can't get to your business information, but simply that your non-marketing posts would not have a clear call to action where you are asking for business or posting the link. Use your About section or bio to tell them about your business, not your posts. When they like what you are saying they will click through to the About section to find out more.

Now lets talk about the 10% promotional posts. This is where you get to shine a light on your product, host benefits or business opportunity. The easiest way to create a promotional post is to share something from your home office's social media sites. Their social media presence is often a great resource for you to use for this purpose as corporate posts tend to be customer-outreach oriented and more marketing in nature. Simply use the share link on the post, being sure to select the correct destination (your Business Page for example) and then always add your own thoughts or caption in order to bring the expertise back to you as your readers' Consultant. Since this is a promotional post it is also a good idea to paste in your own personal website link, to make sure your readers can easily find the item you are promoting.

When creating your own posts though, try to use a picture if you can (something eye-catching but not full of text—those are perceived as spammy.) If you cannot take your own picture or create it using existing marketing images that your company might provide, go to a royalty-free image site and use one of the ones that are allowable for commercial purposes. These are sometimes free, and sometimes there is a charge of about $1 to use them. One I use a lot for free images is Pixabay. You can use them for any reason and they are great. So for example if you are promoting an opportunity meeting, you can search on Pixabay for images for "business meeting" or "women business," and download the picture you want to use in your post, adding your caption about your opportunity meeting in the post. Just be sure not to inadvertently "steal" someone else's image. See my chapter, Avoiding Litigation When Posting Images (page 113) for more information. No one wants you or your company to get into hot water for misusing images.

Whenever possible make the caption of your promotional post about the reader and their needs, not about you and how awesome your special is. Think of a way to word your post so that you are giving them information about how they will benefit if they say yes to you. I like to mix it up a little with questions and statements. So in the example about the opportunity meeting, the caption might be something like, "How many of you are now thinking about how you will be paying all your holiday bills? Do you wish you could have a debt-free Christmas just once in your life? I did too, and I am so grateful I found ABC company. If you want to learn how starting your own home-based business can ease your money worries, join me this Monday for a complimentary info call about joining ABC company. No obligation, just information to help you decide if you'd like to do what I'm doing!"

The idea is to be casual, conversational and pressure-free, helping the reader put his or herself into the picture of using your product or service, or joining your team, augmented with the actual picture you chose. These types of post work great because it is clear you are trying to HELP.

I understand that some of you may not have a budget for promoting your posts or may even be prohibited from paying for advertising. However, if you are able to, consider paying once in a while to promote your one "sales-y" post. Almost all of the social media sites now have some form of sponsored posts, but the most affordable I have found is on Facebook. When you have something to promote and you really want to make sure it is seen, it pays to "boost" your post or even create a targeted ad. I have found that boosting a post for as little as $1 greatly increases my results. If you are following the 9-1-1 Code and maybe posting eleven times a week, one of those would be a promotional post. Pay to boost that one post for a week for just $1.00 and your advertising budget would still only be $4.00 a month. For the results I am seeing, I think it is worth a try if you are able to.

As for the one casual or personal post, the idea behind that is that once in a while it is a good idea to let people in on more of your personality as a consultant or leader. Let them know who you are in some way by sharing something more personal or casual. Be careful not to overdo it. Be professional, but let them see the more casual side of you. This will help build trust and rapport. I like to do this on Sundays when I am "off duty," or occasionally I will have something like a "Fun Friday" post. Here are some guidelines when it comes to personal posts:

DO: Share about the non-business side of your life once in a while: Where you are going; what you are doing. Share a quote that is meaningful to you, or ask a question that everyone can chime in on. Share personal pictures; tell your story. Keep things positive, although occasionally showing your vulnerability or a personal challenge is okay, too. Try to focus on the big picture or put a positive spin on your challenge, so people who are reading it are inspired.

DON'T: Bring in politics, religion, race, sex, sports or other polarizing topics. Use your manners and create conversations like you would in a truly social situation. When sharing something very personal, avoid getting too hung up on the details and focus more on the outcome or overarching lesson learned. And don't forget the old saying, "Don't post anything online that you wouldn't want on the 6 o'clock news!"

Overall, you will reach more people when your business posts are subtle and engaging. Give your readers what they want to hear, something they would look forward to reading every day whether or not they are doing business with you.

The time frame in which the 9-1-1 Code posts occur does not matter as much as the proper ratio. For example, the eleven posts could happen across the span of eleven days, or across a week. Or in weeks when you really have a lot to say, they could occur within a couple of days. The proportion of posts is what matters — make sure you are always much heavier on the non-marketing messages.

As of this printing, the average Facebook user has about 350 friends. When you post on your social media site, and your customer likes your post, your business is potentially exposed to that person's 350 friends. If your customer liked it so much that she shares that same post to her own Facebook network, not only did her 350 friends potentially see it, but when any of her friends like or comment on the post she shared, their 350 friends might see it, too. That's powerful! That kind of engagement doesn't happen if your posts are overly promotional.

I tried to be more consistent in implementing my products into every-day life. Some examples: (1) The stress of helping my son with his school project, Algebra 1 homework, studying for a test, etc. Thank goodness I have my energy supplement for those stressful times. (2) I might show a picture of a high calorie "cheat day" meal with my bottle of weight loss product next to the plate. These show people some real life examples of how they might use our products.

Tina Sanchez,

It Works Independent Consultant

instagram.com/tina_wrapsplusmore/

Finding Your Social Media Voice

As I mentioned in the previous chapter, it is recommended that when marketing your business in social media, to not post primarily promotional messages such as "buy my product" every day. This offends your audience and gives them a sense that you are only there to "get" and not to "give" or be social.

Consumers respond best when your social media posts—business or personal—are useful and relevant to them in some way, whether or not they do business with you as a result. As they get to know you more through your posts, and come to understand that you care about them, interact, and want to provide useful content, they start to look forward to your posts. When trust and rapport are well-established, they are more likely to purchase, join or send a referral your way.

However, for most of us, this presents a challenge in developing posts on a regular basis that are compelling and engaging. We are faced with striking a balance between personal sharing and business promotion, while allowing a sense of both privacy and authenticity at the same time. How can we decide what to post to be of service and truly engage with our readers, while at the same time build our businesses?

Here are ten questions to keep in mind when considering content to post or share when using social media marketing:

1. What is your personal persona or avatar? If someone were to ask another person what you are like, what would they say?

2. What is your business persona or avatar? What comes to mind for others when they think of your business or describe you as a representative of that company to others?

3. What are your five core personal values that you wish to uphold and exemplify in your day-to-day living? See the next chapter for an exercise to help determine these.

4. What are five core business values that form the backbone of your business as an entrepreneur ?

5. What are five to ten challenges that your ideal customer or prospect face for which you might have a solution?

6. What is the level of importance or priority they would place on overcoming these challenges?

7. What, related to your customers' challenges, are topics they can learn about on their own, or with minimal guidance, in some way?

8. Which of your customers' challenges are areas that you, your product or your opportunity can "fix" for them?

9. What are the obstacles, objections, or push-back that you or your customers might encounter when attempting to solve their problems?

10. What are five to ten resources you have at your disposal to share with your customers or prospects?

By answering these questions, you will be able to consider topics of relevance and interest that your readers appreciate and with which they are more likely to engage. Then ask yourself, does the content you are about to send reflect well on your own values and business goals? When you have congruence, your voice in social media will stand out, support your business, and get results!

My business is built exclusively on awesome people. I love awesome people. It's a law of attraction that like seeks like. And in this case, awesome seeks awesome. Sounds like a bad personals ad, right?

But there's a lot of truth to that. Call it the Universe, call it a greater power, call it whatever you like. The fact remains that the energy you put out into the world is reflected back to you ten-fold.

Social media allows me to be a magnet to this never-ending supply of awesome people. If you think there aren't that many awesome people out there, come hang out with me for a few days. I'll change your mind.

Whether I'm out and about or on Facebook, Twitter, Pinterest, Instagram — you name it, I find the greatest people to be friends with. And that's been incredible for my business and online parties.

A lot of people will tell you that there's a secret sauce to successfully operate on social media. Sure, there's all kinds of tips and tricks to make you a better user — skills and efficiency are incredibly important. You need those tips and tricks to put yourself out there. But if you want to attract the awesome, you have to let your "awesome" shine. Put your flag out there and wave it loud and proud!

What works for me is that I know who I am, and I have a voice. I'm snarky. I love really bad jokes. I love telling stories. I have a song lyric for every situation under the sun. I'm likely to get on a roll telling story after story after story. I'm the person you meet that you feel like we've known each other forever. And I let that come through in my social media presence. I'm me. And I make friends when I use social media. That's my secret sauce. I try to be the person I want to be friends with, and then I try to be a really good friend.

When I do an online party, I want it to be as much fun as is humanly possible. I want Suzy's boss to give her the stink eye from across the office because she's giggling while she sneaks a peek at the party on Facebook when she's supposed to be doing the books.

Sure, I have a script for my parties so that I remember to introduce everything. But it's more of an outline and I mix it up. I make it my own and I customize it for my host. I also cross collateralize my material. You have a wish list? Oh, I made a Pinterest Board with what you like — just for you. I mix my media. I keep it highly visual. I use music, video, stills, live feeds — you name it. You have a favorite team? How about a Flipagram video with items in your team's colors set to your school's fight song?

My parties are a mixed media smorgasbord across multiple social media platforms. I have even been known to teach dance lessons during my parties. I use YouTube tutorials and a live feed. Does that have anything to do with what I'm selling? Nope. Is it fun? Oh yeah.... Cue the song from Ferris Bueller's Day Off... OHHHHH YEAHHHHH!!! Chick — a chick-KAH!!!

Next time you're on Twitter, do a hashtag search for one of your company's popular products. I bet you'll find a lot of the same corporate images over and over again with the same boring copy that says something like "buy this, and you get this." Well, it's awesome the first few times it's shared. And then it's just old material. It's actually kind of boring. "Ain't Nobody Got Time For That!"

But what they do have time for is ME. I show them my style. I create my own images. I make my own videos. I make my own media that showcases what it is that I bring to the table. And you can too! Don't know how? Ask Karen Clark! She'll make sure you know how to do this from A-Z!

Social media is the mouthpiece that I use to express myself. I'm creative. I let my freak flag fly. And I let my friends and customers know that when they party with me, they are in for a treat. Why? Because they are getting ME, and I put on a show. Oh, and they get some awesome product too!

Jennifer H. Quisenberry,
Jamberry Independent Consultant
twitter.com/ninjaofnails

Your Business Values

When I was first asked about my personal and business "core values" I thought that I was pretty in touch and that they would be easy to list. I was surprised at the daunting task it actually was to put down on paper the values I and my business represent. To help you discover what is most important to you and your business, so that you can better develop posts for your social media marketing, I've listed some below.

Do the following exercise and you will gain clarity on how to develop content to share with your readers that is a reflection of who you are, personally and professionally.

1. Circle twenty values (on the next page) that are important to you.

2. Imagine you had to give up ten of those forever. Cross out ten and keep the ten priorities.

3. Now that you have your top ten, you are only allowed to keep five. These five are the values that even if your life and business depended on it (they do!) you would never give them up! These are your CORE values.

Accountability	Fairness	Patience
Achievement	Family	Perseverance
Adaptability	Financial stability	Professional growth
Ambition	Forgiveness	Personal fulfillment
Attitude	Freedom	Personal growth
Awareness	Friendships	Philanthropy
Balance	Generosity	Power
Being the best	Growth	Recognition
Caring	Health	Reliability
Change	Honesty	Religion
Coaching	Humility	Reputation
Community	Humor/fun	Respect
Competence	Independence	Responsibility
Commitment	Influence	Risk-taking
Community	Initiative	Safety
Compassion	Integrity	Self-discipline
Competence	Intellect	Self-respect
Conflict resolution	Intuition	Serenity
Cooperation	Involvement	Sophistication
Courage	Job security	Stability
Creativity	Leadership	Status
Dialogue	Legacy	Success
Ease	Listening	Teamwork
Ecology	Location	Time freedom
Enthusiasm	Making a difference	Trust
Entrepreneurism	Mentoring	Vision
Environmental	Nature	Wealth
Efficiency	Open communication	Well-being
Ethics	Openness	Wisdom
Excellence	Order	Work ethic

One thing I've done has been to participate in groups where at a particular evening and time, everyone gets online and shares five minutes about their product/company. It's the same group every week, one rep per company, and therefore people really got to know, like, and trust each other. Whenever I thought of a particular company I would think of the rep I met through this program and place an order through her. We'd tell each other when specials were happening, purchase from each other, and develop friendships.

Heather Price,

Independent Beauty Consultant, Mary Kay

facebook.com/heatheramypricedotcom

Social Media Post Ideas

Social media profiles are relatively simple to start, and as you gain experience and confidence you can add powerful customizations. Best of all, most are highly indexed by the major search engines due to their popularity and the fact that they are constantly refreshed and have an incredible link structure around them (links going in and out). Creating your social media profiles is the easy part. One of the most common questions I get though, is what to post on them once they are created!

One of the easiest ways to come up with what to say or how to BE in social media marketing is to think about these two questions before you write your post.

What do you want your readers to do at the end of reading your post? and *How do you want people to feel?*

Begin with the end in mind. If you want them to take action by reading more on a link you provide, then the way you present it needs to compel them to want to know more — out of curiosity or a desire to learn. If you want them to like the post or share it with their friends, then ideally the post is something that creates a sense of advocacy or service, in that your readers learned something new or were inspired so much that they want to share that feeling with others. If you want them to participate in a discussion and comment on the post, they need to feel connected to you and the topic and to desire being in community with you and your other readers. Ask them a question! Encourage them to express themselves.

Social media has devolved in some sense to where people only post superficial things like what they are having for dinner, instead of truly connecting. Businesses post mostly about their special offers, their new products, or run flashy contests to build a "buzz" they think will grow their businesses. Why do we do that? It's because it is easy. It's because it's what we know. It's because we are protecting ourselves from being vulnerable and open, from being who we are. But why? It is human nature to fear rejection. The irony is that by avoiding authenticity in your communication you risk getting exactly that—rejection! People can sense when you are inauthentic.

So I am calling for a shift in how we handle social media marketing, and in using social media in general. Just as in other marketing trends in recent years, consumers are ready for a shift toward **humanity** in marketing. We see this in television commercials that are evolving into more storytelling vignettes, almost like mini-movies! We see this in print ads that are depicting more lifestyle images of real people, rather than perfect studio photo shoots. We see this in the rise in popularity of video and live-streaming where people grab their smart phone and broadcast their thoughts and ideas freely to anyone who will listen. Why has this not translated to how entrepreneurs market themselves online? We have gotten so caught up in the **doing** that we've lost track of the **being**.

How can we bring the humanity back into social media for direct selling? How can we get connected, and then stay connected and keep relationships going? In my opinion, it is all about the emotional connection and staying in alignment with your, and your business's core values, always being sensitive to the needs of your customers.

Remembering the 9-1-1 Code and the values exercise in the previous chapter, here is a quick list of ideas you can write about on your social media profiles that will help get your creative thought process going. These posts can supplement what you might already be posting in the way of photos, videos, links to outside articles, questions you would like some feedback on or that you think will spark discussion, or just updating people with what you have been up to in your business. Perhaps you will want to keep a notebook of post ideas, or put this up on the wall near your computer for when you are having a social media "writer's block!"

Post Ideas

1. Where are you going? (Related to your business — not "to the grocery store")

2. Who are you seeing? (See above!)

3. What projects are you working on? Can you give a teaser?

4. Tell what you are reading that has to do with a topic relevant to your business.

5. Let people know about any related videos you are watching.

6. What have you been doing in your business since the last news update you posted?

7. Share about someone you admire in your field, company, or industry.

8. Share about someone who influenced you in business or as a person.

9. Have a Customer of the Day, Host of the Day or Team Member of the Day — tell the world how great they are.

10. Read blogs in your industry and share interesting articles regularly. Use a tool such as Feedly or Flipboard to scan headlines when you need an idea.

11. Share an inspiring quotation, and an explanation of how it applies to your business.

12. Share a funny anecdote about something that happened in your business or at a party or event.

13. Ask your readers what they are working on or excited about.

14. Tell what inspires you and ask your readers what inspires them, too.

15. Share a quick how-to. Even the simplest things need explanation and people appreciate that! Something you take for granted every day could be a lifesaver when someone new learns how to do it.

16. Post a photograph of your product.

17. Post a photo of a creative use for your product.

18. Post a photograph of you or a customer using your product.

19. Post a video demonstrating one aspect of your product.

20. Post a video explaining an aspect of your business.

21. Post pictures of customers attending your events.

22. Post links to your other websites, blogs, or social media pro-files.

23. Did you catch a TV show that is related in some way to your business? Tell your readers, so they can watch for it too. Share your opinion and/or ask a question about it.

24. Share your favorite books related to your business—and why.

25. Review related products or services and make recommendations to your readers.

26. Ask your readers for their recommendations about related products or services.

27. Give your readers an opportunity to serve you—ask for help, show them you're human too!

28. Share about events or teleclasses your readers may want to participate in.

29. Share a funny cartoon or picture related to your topic.

30. Share a news article related to your topic.

31. Make up a Top 10 List about something and post it.

32. Write a "Why I Love..." post. Could be about your town, a person, a business, or a product.

33. Share useful tools you use in your business, and where to find them.

34. Share your favorite website resources.

35. Share some Do's and Don'ts about your product or service.

36. Share a memory related to your business – and ask your readers to share theirs.

37. Share about why you started your business.

38. Share about your early days starting the business.

39. Post about clubs or Meetup groups you belong to.

40. Post your "in a perfect world" wish list.

41. Post a "Question of the Day" or Week.

42. Take a poll about a mildly controversial topic (ex: Coke vs. Pepsi)

43. Answer a frequently asked question.

44. Share (and tag) other social media pages you participate in.

45. Post your latest blog posts or go back and post old "favorites."

46. Post when your company adds a new product or service.

47. Post a note of encouragement.

48. Give tips that have helped you succeed.

49. Share ideas for saving money related to your products.

50. Offer creative ideas for having fun related to your products.

51. Post a special for social media followers only – they need to contact you for a discount.

52. Post about an event you are hosting or participating in.

53. Post about the item or service you sell the least of – and tell them why it is a hidden treasure.

54. Post a little-known fact, trick or gimmick related to your product or service.

55. Challenge your readers to take action on something, and then have them post that they have done it in the comments.

56. Post a photo and ask your readers to add a caption.

57. Ask your readers what their favorite book is related to a particular topic.

58. Ask your readers what their plans are for the weekend or their next vacation.

59. Explain one obstacle you had when starting your business or using your product in the beginning—ask them what theirs was.

60. Let them share their personal website, blog, or information about their own lives or businesses once in a while.

Using Questions for Post Ideas

Every business owner receives questions from customers, prospects, clients and networking connections. Why not use those questions as prompts for your social media, video, or blog post ideas? The next time someone asks you a question about your product, your service, about how to do something within your expertise, or anything related to your topic, save that question and begin to build a bank of topic ideas that are customized to you, your topic, and what YOUR market needs to know.

When you are looking for ideas of what to post to social media, pull from that bank of questions, and answer them! Your audience will tell you what they need. You just need to listen. Often you will get the same question over and over. This is a clue that it would serve others to discuss this topic publicly. Chances are, there are hundreds or thousands of more people out there who were wondering the same thing, and maybe

Googling it. When you address the question on your social media channels, your post will win big in the search engines!

Any time I get a question on my Facebook Business Page, or via private message, or by email or phone, I either create a post addressing it, or I queue it up for later posting. Often I am already creating the content for the post when I give the person my answer anyway, so why not repurpose that. This is an easy way to come up with new content. Pay attention to the questions being asked. When you run out of questions, ask a question asking for questions! People love to receive free advice from a reliable source.

Using Social Media to Inspire

Often in my speaking and training I talk about how social media should be used not just for promoting your business, but also to serve existing customers or clients, help people solve problems, or to share ideas and resources. One of my favorite things to give and receive in social media, and on Facebook in particular, is inspiration!

You can use social media to inspire people in a couple of different ways. One way is to post an uplifting quotation from your favorite author or motivational speaker. This sparks your readers' imaginations and often you'll find the very person who needed to read your message today got it. Reading something inspirational, especially if they are just checking in on Facebook to kill time, can often completely change someone's outlook for the day. I know it has for me! I frequently change course after reading a quote that really hit home.

Another way to use social media to inspire people is by sharing what you do, love, or are passionate about! When you post about your big kitchen remodel project and share the ups and downs and then photos of the finished product with your

Facebook friends, they are inspired to work on their own home improvement projects. When you share your travel photos, they are inspired to step outside their safe and comfortable hometown and dream about traveling the world. When you share a cute story about your kids and what they are up to, it inspires them to go spend time with their own children and appreciate every day with them. When you share your success stories, they celebrate along with you and are inspired to reach for their own goals.

For those who have not been posting much on social networking sites because you just can't think of what to say, or you wonder why anyone would want to read what you are up to, think again. If you look at using social media to inspire people, it has more meaning and is so rewarding when you understand you are touching people's lives in a positive way. Go on, post something!

I started using Facebook full blown when I started with my business. What I found was that I was able to see who in my friends list or their friends list might benefit from what I had to offer. I created friendships, amusing posts and of course posted about my job. I have found that through the years more people know what I do and who I am. I try to keep most of my business posts to not feel like am selling but sharing. Just from sharing, I have locked in fundraisers, orders and parties — both Facebook and home parties.

I was recently at a BBQ with my husband at one of his friend's homes and a lady came up to me and said, "You do PartyLite, right?" Oh, yes I do! Well, that turned into an $800 party with three bookings and you can imagine the many contacts and other bookings from *that!! This just from someone I never met other then being a Facebook Friend until that day. I love my social media platforms!!*

Arilys Palacios,
Independent PartyLite Consultant
facebook.com/arilysp

Measuring Social Media's ROI
(Return on Interaction)

Measuring your ROI (Return on Investment) in business is a standard practice for any business owner or entrepreneur who wants to become and stay profitable. Knowing the specific monetary results that come from your investments of time and money guides your business decisions.

When it comes to online social networking, however, there are gray areas that often make people uncomfortable. Business owners are wondering where is the return? When is this going to pay off? And, most of all, is this worth my time and money when I have other measurable marketing strategies I can use? How do I know if it is working if I cannot measure dollars coming in against dollars going out?

With social media marketing, the return is not on the investment—**the return is on the interaction**. You do not put in money to get more money—you put in interaction to get more interaction, which returns tenfold in trust, loyalty and the development of relationships that become customers and advocates for your business.

When you invest in interactions, the results are an increased number of email newsletter subscriptions, Twitter followers, Facebook fans, or blog comments. From there, you can typically track an increase in the number of product orders, new clients or referrals.

The types of statistics you will want to collect and compare will depend on the original goals and objectives you have set for your activity in social media. Here are some of the analytics tools that can help you get started in understanding where you stand with your interactions online:

- Facebook Page Insights: *facebook.com/insights* (must have at least 30 likes)

- LinkedIn Profile Stats: *linkedin.com/wvmx/profile*

- Twitter Analytics: *analytics.twitter.com*

- Analytics for Pinterest: *analytics.pinterest.com* (must convert to business account)

- Instagram Statistics by Iconosquare: *iconosquare.com/*

When I first came to Facebook I was only on there to chat with friends. One day I came across an ad for a weight loss supplement and thought, "Oh geez, not another one."

I knew all too well that they never work. After a few days of watching and seeing it over and over again on Facebook I decided to take the plunge and give it a shot. After a few days one of the girls asked me if I wanted to become a Distributor and sell it. I had no idea how to do any of that since I worked in mortgages.

I decided to give it a shot....Who doesn't need to make some extra money, right? I followed what she did and kept at it each day. I started a weight loss group on Facebook and posted for my friends to join and pass around the news. It seemed that it wasn't going as great as I thought it would and was very close to quitting. My friend talked me out of it and said she had faith in my and that I could do this and be successful with it. I told myself that I was going to wake up with determination and make this work.

As of today I have been with the company for over 2 1/2 years and have over 16,000 members in my weight loss group. I enjoy working from home and waking up with that determination — it is why I am where I am today.

Marcine Jenis,

Prüvit

facebook.com/marcine.jenis1

Scheduling and Automation

In my opinion scheduling posts is something you should do only occasionally, not every day, all day. Your followers can tell when you've checked out and are using an outside tool. Some might argue that scheduling everything is better than not posting at all. I disagree. To develop an engaged and loyal following, use scheduling tools sparingly, if at all. In fact a recent study claimed that in Facebook, posts that originate from an outside scheduling application receive 89% less engagement than posts which are started from within Facebook. That is something to pay attention to and really consider whether using a scheduler is necessary. Sometimes it really helps though, so I wanted to be sure to mention the options that are out there for you.

For example, you may want to schedule all of your 6 am posts, or all of your 8 pm posts, if you find those are good times for your readers. However I do not recommend that you do that, and then never check back in "live." Or perhaps you would choose to schedule your weekend posts, but not your weekday posts. Here's another example: I live in California and

I typically have an early morning post, but I set it to go out while I am taking my son to school. When I return, I am able to check in and reply to any comments or add other thoughts. I only use a scheduler for that one because if I wait until I return, it would be almost noon Eastern time, which, for my audience, is a little late for me to get started. In addition, if I've already posted a few times in a day, but I think of something new to post, I might use a scheduler in order to add my new post to the "queue" while I am thinking about it. Again I am always sure to go back and check for the conversation occurring around that post.

Always, always, always reply to comments directed to you. Even if you are away for a while and schedule posts during a trip, check back in on those previous posts when you return and address any comments or replies. If you schedule an early morning post, go back in later in the day to check for things that need your attention.

Another thing to consider is to be ready to cancel any scheduled posts across the networks if there is a nationwide or global tragedy or other crisis. For example, when the Boston Marathon bombing occurred in 2013, many businesses were inadvertently still posting "happy" social media posts, as if nothing had happened, even though the rest of the Internet was grieving. You must be prepared to go back and cancel your scheduled posts in such cases.

For Facebook Business Pages, I recommend always using the built-in Schedule calendar. To use this, go to the publishing box where you would normally create your post, and do all that is required to get your post ready. Then instead of using the Publish button, select the small downward arrow next to it and then select Schedule. From there you can choose a date and time you would like your post to go out! Because of the way

Facebook's news feed algorithm works, posts that originate from within your Business Page—instead of from an outside tool—get the most visibility.

Scheduling tools for individuals that you might want to explore for use in Facebook groups or events, or in your other social media such as Twitter, LinkedIn, Pinterest and Instagram include:

- HootSuite

- CinchShare

- Buffer App

- TinyTorch

- PostCron

Your company home office may also have a software solution that they have licensed to use with the field. In these cases, your company is able to create and store social media posts and images—or templates for posts—so that consultants can schedule posts to their social media profiles. If your company is providing this for you, great! I do recommend whenever possible, that you still customize the caption to reflect your own thoughts and enthusiasm so that the social media sites—and readers—understand it is a unique post from an individual. Posting hundreds or thousands of the exact same thing from many consultants is something that could possibly trigger a "Facebook Jail" situation. See my chapter on How to Avoid Facebook Jail on page 99.

Organic Social Media

Despite the title, this chapter is not about food — it is about being natural in your social media efforts. Lately I have seen more and more people trying to "game the system" to grow the number of followers and fans they have on Facebook, Instagram, Twitter or other social media sites. Sometimes it's as easy as paying someone a small fee to "guarantee" thousands of followers. As tempting as this is, especially when you are starting, I would encourage you to grow your following more organically — and then be patient.

To be long-lasting and effective in marketing through social media, this cannot be a numbers game. I personally am not in a race to have more Business Page "likes" than my competition. In fact, when you have many connections on your Page who do not also interact, your visibility in the News Feed actually goes down because there's an unnatural imbalance. I also learned the hard way my first go-around that more followers on Twitter does not mean more business — it just means more noise.

Marketing your business and building an online presence through social media should be about connecting with people, not collecting people. Think about your "in real life" networking events. Which is a more effective networking strategy — going around and collecting everyone's business cards? Adding everyone on the attendee list to your email newsletter? Or do you achieve better results if you take the time to get to know a few key people, and then have some two-way conversations?

Quality over quantity is what works best in real life, and the same is true for your online presence.

Be the kind of person in your online social networking that you would be in your real life networking, and people will be naturally attracted to you; they will naturally refer others to you; and they will naturally want to find out more about you and want to work with you.

How do you do this?

- **Show up**. Every day. Maybe not on all of the social media platforms, but pick your favorite and show up every day.

- **Be of service**. Put others first and freely give the information, advice, resources, and support that they need.

- **Ask questions.** Get to know your friends, fans and followers' thoughts, feelings, opinions, and needs by asking questions. Give them an opportunity to share about themselves or their businesses.

- **Be relevant.** When you post, use words and phrases that people who need exactly what you have to offer would be using in the search engines. Use SEO-oriented keyword searches that will help you tweak your language if necessary. Make it easy for your future customers and prospects to find you!

- **Be picky.** Choose who you want to work with. Be proactive and seek out or accept social media connections that you feel would be complimentary to your values, goals, and ideals. You don't have to do business with everyone who has a pulse. Remember that everyone in your social circle online can see everyone else you're associated with and their behavior. Do you want to be associated with people whose values contradict your own? When you befriend, follow or fan someone in social media, it is an implied recommendation — so be choosey.

- **Be social.** Interact. Respond. Follow up. This is critical! At a networking event would you ignore someone's comment, question, or request? Would you look the other way, or start talking to someone else? Of course not! Check for comments and replies directed to you and respond — always.

- **Be patient.** I don't know if it is due to the nature of the Internet and that we expect instant answers these days, but people expect immediate results. Slow down — calm down — be patient! Do you want a stable, loyal, secure, and solid customer base who will be with you for years and continue referring others to you at least that long? Then be patient. Let things grow organically, develop that rapport and loyalty over time, and the trust that you will build will be unshakable.

Marketing your business online is best when taken in small steps, consistently over time. Slow and steady truly does win the race, and those who build a following naturally, ethically and with service are those who find lasting success.

One of my good friends — and now current team members — came from connecting through social media. We were in a Facebook group due to a mutual interest, but nothing related to my business. We became Facebook friends, and she saw my occasional posts about my business. Eventually she wanted to know more, so we met at a Starbucks and she made a purchase.

She later hosted a party (more than once), and after a couple of years of shopping and hosting, I finally persuaded her to join my team. Now we are friends, our kids are friends, and it's all good!

I have also met several other friends now through local moms' groups on Facebook, and it has opened the door, not only to new friendships, but also to sharing my products and opportunity with them.

Sandy Kreps,
Independent Scentsy/Velata Consultant
facebook.com/sandysellsscents

Customer Service Through Social Media

One of the simplest, yet most rewarding, things you can do in social media is to serve your customers. Serve — as in "give." Be there for them. It's not a novel concept, especially when it comes to sales/direct selling — this is what we do best in "real life" situations. It's all about the customer, the relationship and fostering loyalty through service. When it comes to the social media landscape, this simple concept is one that actually can set an individual entrepreneur apart from the competition, the big box stores — as well as the online giants — and make your business thrive.

In a recent survey, it was found that one-third of people who contact businesses on social media *never get a response.* Is it difficult to respond? It is if you have a "set it and forget it" approach to social media. It isn't if you have a human-to-human, relationship-building approach to social media. If you had a brick and mortar storefront where you sold your products, and a customer came to the counter to ask a question or to return an item, would you simply stare at them, or look the other way? Or worse, start talking about something else entirely, to all within earshot? No, of course not. But when a customer connects with you online, for some reason many — in fact, too many — businesses ignore them.

Here are some simple ways you can stand out by paying attention to **serving** your customers online:

1. Simply respond to comments, private messages, or wall posts directed to you. If you are following my Social Media CPR formula, this is a daily task you are implementing already. It doesn't take long. Do it.

2. Respond whether the comments were positive or negative in nature.

3. Personalize and humanize your response: What would you say if this person were standing in front of you? How would you behave? Would you use their name? Would you thank them? How can you make sure the exchange is a positive one?

4. You may wish to reply to them privately and work on finding a solution that way, but it is critical that you still respond publicly (We will send you a private message — please check your inbox!), so that other readers can see you are serving that customer.

5. When possible, include other avenues to contact you in your response. Example: "If you have any further questions please feel free to call us at 123-456-7890 or email customer-service@abc.com."

6. Never leave a comment ignored. If there is nothing specific that needs to be said, or there are many broad or general comments, then at the very least at the end of a comment thread, you, since it is your business, can reply to everyone

as the last comment, in order to wrap up the conversation. This shows you are hands-on and attentive, and actually read the comments.

With over 60% of consumers saying that they have used social media for customer service-related communication, it pays to pay attention and perhaps rethink your social strategy. Setting your content up to auto-post and then checking in once a week no longer works if you are a business that wants to serve, stand out, and make a difference with your customers.

I am always thankful for online sales. Quite frequently I will get a website order from a person that I do not know. I feel it is very important to always follow-up with those customers with a Thank You note, as well as a phone call if possible to make sure that they receive their products and that everything was in good condition. Many times I have ordered online from a website of a home-based business and never heard a single word from that person to thank me. If I do not feel important I will not order from them again.

I want my customers to know that they are important to me and that I appreciate them. A simple phone call or a Thank You note are easy ways to keep your online customers, no matter how far away they live from you.

Jennifer Allen,
Gold Canyon candles
pinterest.com/wixnstix

People Before Things

I am happy to say that on the Internet lately, I see a trend of "people before things" emerging. The techniques that worked yesterday—flashy websites with big bold graphics, squeeze pages that read like infomercials, and repetitive messaging to get noticed—are no longer very effective. A focus on the people—not the product, the customer—not the bottom line, is emerging. Social media and general online marketing should be about connecting with people, not collecting people.

The rapid growth of mainstream social media for marketing over the last few years has been a precursor to this trend. Customers want to be spoken with, not spoken to. They want to receive a response from a live person, not a canned form letter. They want to engage with business owners and know that if an issue arises, they will be treated with genuine service, not treated like a number.

Pay very special attention to this trend, because in this economy, when customers and prospects are more choosy than ever about where they spend their hard-earned dollars, putting "people before things" is what will make you stand out, and it is what will bring your customers back to you over and over.

Here are six ways to think about putting people before things in the online marketing efforts:

1. **Remember the golden rule, always.** Treat others the way you'd like to be treated. That is the golden rule. We grow up hearing this, and yet when it comes to online marketing, many business owners forget that. I prefer the version that says to treat others the way they would like to be treated. Be courteous, kind, honest, and respectful of your customers and readers. Offer a superior service or product that will benefit their lives, and promote it to them in a respectful and courteous manner, so that they are open to hearing your message and sharing it with others.

2. **Speak when spoken to.** Customers today want to know that a live person is behind the website or email marketing campaign. Respond to their questions or comments. Check your Facebook Page for comments, and reply, answer your @ replies on Twitter, and engage in conversation through other social media site comments. There is nothing worse for your online presence than customer feedback or questions that go unanswered — publicly.

3. **Honesty is the best policy.** One of the buzzwords in online business is "transparency," and that means being forthcoming and honest with your customers whenever possible. Being up front about delays or changes builds trust and loyalty. Manipulating your customers and using marketing tricks to increase your numbers doesn't work any more. To gain quality, targeted customers who are loyal to you, it's time to get real.

4. **Measure twice. Cut once.** While we are being honest, and interactive, and respectful, we also need to maintain a positive professional image online. Since the nature of online marketing today leans toward social, be sure that you are presenting yourself and your company with the exact impression you want to make. Chances are, if you make a mistake, it will quickly get spread by word of mouth through social networking, and you will spend a lot of time cleaning up the mess afterward. Proofread your responses, or better yet, have a second pair of eyes double check your written communication. Check for writing conventions, but also for tone and voice. Do your homework and research an issue before posting or responding to a customer.

5. **Your word is your bond.** In today's world, integrity is everything. For years now, customers have been let down by businesses, organizations and government—and they will not tolerate it any more. They will simply choose another company or representative to patronize. Do what you say you will do, when you say you will do it. Keep agreements with your customers and follow through on requests. Appearing flaky— especially in the public eye of social media, even for a moment—will result in damage to your reputation and losing your customer to someone else.

6. **Knowledge talks, wisdom listens.** It used to be that it was critical to present yourself as an expert in your field; declare your knowledge and impart it to them over and over until it sinks in. Now, it is critical to be an expert with your customers. Get to know them. Listen to them. Find out what their needs are and offer solutions to them. Listen to them. The questions that come up most often from your customers can become your next social media posts. The comments

you receive can lead to improvements in your product or service. The thank you notes or praise you collect can be used as feedback about what you're doing right — take note of it and do more of it. Listen to your customers and they'll notice.

"People before things" is a saying you may have heard long ago. It is a concept that is tried and true in relationships in the "real world" and your customers and fellow representatives will be happy to see it emerging as one of the best practices of online marketing. When direct sellers put people first, the rewards are solid and long-lasting.

I was receiving leads from my company website for new customers and recruits from all across the country and I thought it was a glitch in the company's system. After talking at length to two team members, I discovered that following Karen's tips on Facebook Business Page postings, as well as other websites such as Google and LinkedIn, that I had leveraged myself to the top of search engines. It's absolutely clear and a no brainer to link my Facebook page in the about me section to my Business Page instead of the main Facebook page for my direct selling company but I would not have known that it was even possible without Karen's help!

Kimberly Bolton,
Independent Direct Selling Leader
facebook.com/mylittleorganizerbag

Avoid
Common Problems

Don't Be Boring

I see so many consultants that are just plain boring on social media. I hate to say it but consumers do not want to see ten pictures of your products every day on your Business Page, nor do they want to see constant coupons, contests and "campaigns" promoting your business. This is a people business. It's about relationships. You know that.

Actually, so often I hear people saying they love "so-and-so's" Facebook page because they **aren't** just promoting all the time.

When a customer or prospect likes your Facebook page, or engages on any of your social media sites, they already like your products. Sure, they want to hear about them once in a while and catch what's new or a special deal, but not four times a day every day of the week. It's boring. Consumers don't like it.

Instead, give your readers a **window into your world** as a direct seller. Show them what you are up to. Take a picture of yourself getting orders ready. Did you go to an event? Show us! Did you hold an in-home party? Share a snapshot. Did you visit a local customer or host? Take a picture of her! Those things are interesting. They humanize your business and help people feel connected to you on a deeper level than simply loving your products.

Always have your smart phone ready to snap a picture of an excited customer, a home party gathering that shows how fun they are, the ladies going crazy cheering each other at your team meeting, or your view from the local holiday vendor boutique. Ask people in the picture if it's okay to share on social media. Take a picture of your home office, a special organizing tool you use, or your favorite business book. Show prospects you are a resource for developing a thriving home-based business.

There are creative and compelling moments happening all day long that simply need to be captured and shared! Don't be shy, be SMART and let your readers see what makes you tick as a home-based business person. When you do, you will see your likes, comments, and shares go up. I am sure of it!

A good image gets shared, re-shared and takes on a life of it's own... becomes viral as they say! Everyone has a camera phone these days so there is no reason why you cannot have branded images to share on your social site. Sharing images with your brand or website on them ensures that if someone changes your copy and removes your web link, the image is still branded to you. Believe it or not, unique images are prioritized within search results so a photo that you took and branded may get picked up quicker than an image you re-shared or one that you found online and branded.

Pinterest is totally image-oriented and can be turned into one of your top referral sites on the web (it is mine). So, taking the time to create a system of image branding is worth the effort. When you snap an image on a mobile device that is good enough to share, just immediately brand it with your web URL or company name and a quick quote.

Your phone may have a photo editor that does the job or you can find a photo editor with a few more bells and whistles. I especially like PicArts. Save it for later when you are at a loss as to what to share and you will always have an inventory of unique images.

Another technique to brand images, which is especially handy when looking for something appropriate for a specific blog post or article, is to do a Google search. Don't just grab any image though! There are copyright laws, you know! Google your term then click the image button. After you are on the Google images search page note that on the top of the page there is an option for "License." Click the license button and your drop down will give you choices of copyright labels. (Note: Depending when you read this, the words or choices may change. Just yesterday when I did this, the word choices were different, but you can still use the concept even if the choices change.) Choose: "Free To Modify, Share and Use" You will then be given images that you are allowed to edit and change. The selections will be fewer, but you will never get a notice from a lawyer that you violated copyright laws by reuse of an image.

Catchy images both on your website and in social media will travel the world!!

Deb Bixler,

CashFlowShow.com

pinterest.com/debbixler

Avoid Negative Comments

I tend to "hang out" with a lot of independent consultants who are with direct selling and network marketing companies — both offline and online. They are my friends. They are my clients. They are my fans and followers on social media. Because of this, I hear a lot and see a lot among representatives from various companies on social media. I also see a lot of what is happening in the comments and from their other followers or consumers like me.

Most of the time, the enthusiasm and support is positive. Sometimes, however, the comments are negative, and complain about the social media posts that are posted by a representative of a specific company.

I am not talking about the negative reviews about a company or business opportunity, or someone who trolls the Internet to disparage companies, or the rogue distributors who bash other companies on purpose. Those tend to be handled in other ways with compliance and reputation management.

What I am talking about is when a real consumer, follower, or fan comments negatively about the *social media behavior* of distributors of another company—as a whole. That is correct. Whether it is a few bad apples or an entire organization following a training, negative comments about a distributor's social media behavior are *attributed to the entire company* in one fell swoop.

I am seeing this more and more, and it disturbs me—not so much that a consumer has expressed their frustration in public—that is the way things work now. And in general, it helps keep people accountable for providing good customer service and an excellent product. What disturbs me is that they have something to complain about at all when it comes to social media posts by direct selling consultants.

It's a real problem, because these people aren't going to the company to provide feedback. They aren't even giving individual consultants direct feedback. They are telling their social media connections. It's like they are complaining about you to the world. And in turn, it gives the entire direct selling profession a bad name.

What is the solution? Yes, you can monitor your social media mentions, your Google results and read every post but that will not show you what consumers are saying about your product in closed groups—or to their private network—and it also won't tell you what is being said about your company in general when the brand name isn't mentioned specifically.

The solution is in getting training yourself (like in this book!), and also in training your team in correct ethical social media marketing tactics, so there is nothing to complain about. If your company's representatives are properly trained in setting up social media effectively, and in composing creative social media posts that compel people to interact socially, and trained in knowing when and how often to post, you will be able to eliminate your company's poor reputation. If your company is not already providing this type of training for the field in general, have them get in touch with me. I can help.

The complaints about direct selling social media include:

- Consultants posting promotional content several times a day throughout the week

- Adding hundreds of people to "Facebook party" events without their permission

- Adding hundreds of people to private Facebook groups without their permission

- Doctoring before and after photos and making claims about results or income

- Posting too often and "filling up my feed" with posts about products or opportunities

- Using Instagram to post graphical "ads" instead of photos, which is the purpose of this service

- Adding people to personal social media accounts, only to private message them with spam

Proper social media training—and then implementing what you learn—can make an enormous impact on a company's or team's reputation. It's the best way to avoid negative comments!

How to Avoid "Facebook Jail"

Once in a while it will come to my attention that a consultant, or several of them, have been put in "Facebook Jail." The consultants are suddenly not allowed to post any links to their personal websites or blogs, or to their company-replicated websites—not on their personal timeline, not in Facebook groups and not even on the Business Pages they've created. When they post a link, a notice comes up saying that this domain has been determined to be spam.

I have also heard from distributors that people had their entire Facebook account deleted and had to start completely over from zero. They lose their personal timeline, all their posts, and all their connections. Of course they are devastated and have to spend the next couple months desperately begging people to join their new account.

I also know of several people who have been blocked from adding friends on Facebook, and others who are no longer allowed to send private messages.

These sanctions are upsetting when you consider the amount of time and resources you may be putting into social media marketing. What's more is that Facebook makes it difficult to appeal their decisions or to talk to a live person and explain yourself or even understand why you are suddenly blocked. Following are several ways you can avoid being put in this unfortunate situation.

1. **Understand Facebook's Terms of Service** both for personal Timelines, and for Business Pages. Most sanctions on Facebook can be avoided by following their rules. Unfortunately most people do not read them.

2. **Never ever ever use a business name for a Personal Profile/Timeline name.** You may not create a personal Facebook account using "Susie's Sweet Shop" as the name of the account. Some people will try to do this, to "brand" their personal Facebook or so they can post within groups and elsewhere as the name of their business. This is against the rules on Facebook. Profiles/Timelines are for real people and you need to use your real name. Use your personal name on your personal account, and then within the About section, alert people to your business. Create a Business Page for business.

3. **Each human being on the planet can only have ONE Facebook account.** From your personal account you can create multiple Business Pages but you can only have one personal account. Use your Account Settings to add multiple email addresses to your account if you want to make sure business contacts can find you easily. If you are concerned about privacy on your personal account, use Facebook's built-in functions for Following, Friend and Interest Lists to keep things separate.

4. **Do not post overly promotional items on a personal account.** One of Facebook's rules is that your personal Timeline cannot be used for commercial purposes. There has been some debate about the definition of "commercial" but, in general, when you are sending a marketing message including a link or call to action, it should be from a Business Page, not a personal Timeline. Sure you can talk about what you are doing in your business, you can share images and information, but including a link to where they can buy or sign up crosses the line into promoting, and Facebook wants all of that to occur on Business Pages. Following my 9-1-1 Code, whether on a personal Timeline or Business Page is highly recommended. As a reminder, this code states that your proportion of posts should be nine non-marketing (inform, inspire, educate) to every one promotional post (buy-book-join) along with one personal or casual post.

5. **Avoid posting your web link to multiple places on Facebook in a short time.** When sharing your website or social media website link within Facebook groups or other Pages, even when it is encouraged by the group or Page admin (such as on "Facebook Friday"), avoid doing so in multiple groups in short succession. It is never a good idea to blast your link all over the place on the web anyway — it appears desperate and spammy. But it is common on "Facebook Friday" for groups or pages to ask you to share your link — it helps everyone get to know each other and show support for the other pages. Spread these posts out over time so you aren't doing them all at once. As a side note, I am not in favor of "like ladders" where everyone posting is required to like each others' posts. It can actually damage your visibility

on Facebook to have people like your Page who aren't going to interact with it.

6. **Do not friend-request people you do not know or aren't otherwise connected to.** As I state in almost all of my training, social media is about *connecting with people, not collecting people*. When you have a relationship with someone, either in your real life, or in a Facebook group, and you want to get to know them better, sure, reach out to them, as long as they are someone who would recognize you and value the connection. But if you don't know them or they would not recognize and appreciate the request, do not reach out. The reason for this is that after they ignore your friend request if they do not want to add you back, Facebook asks if they know you. If they say "No," that they do not know you, your account could be flagged as spam. If your account is flagged too many times, you are blocked from sending friend requests, since it appears you are adding people to spam them.

7. **Do not promote your business on other business or personal Timelines or walls without being asked.** Whether it is a "wall post" or a comment, it is not okay to visit another business or Personal Profile and tell their network all about your business. Do not go and like someone's page and then post on their page "New liker from XYZ company, like me back!" either. Do not troll for "openings" on pages and comment with, "You can buy a great XYZ here" and include your link. Would you go into a store and pass out fliers about your store across the street? Besides it just being poor manners, the page admin will likely delete your comment and mark it as spam, flagging your account.

8. **Do not private message someone who is not your Facebook friend.** This is an automatic red flag and although Facebook has a small tolerance for it once in a while, if you do this too often you will surely end up in Facebook jail. The assumption is that if they wanted to receive messages from you, you would be friends. This is similar to the opt-in rules of the CAN-SPAM Act whereby someone needs to acquire written permission to be able to email marketing messages to another. Facebook does not want to get in trouble for spamming any more than you do.

9. **Do not use Facebook Messages to send promotional content to multiple people at once without their consent.** Facebook does allow you to send a message to up to twenty people at a time, but this function is designed for people who all want to discuss something—not for someone to broadcast an advertising message. When you send a group message, every reply or activity on that message is sent as a notification to all twenty people, and this gets annoying fast. Members in the message will click the settings to leave the conversation and mark it as spam. It is against Facebook's rules to send commercial messages to people without their consent.

10. **Do not repeatedly send the same message to different people or post the same item in different places.** This is tracked by Facebook and seen as spam or harassment. If you have a useful, non-commercial message to send (for example, connecting with someone regarding your class reunion) simply vary the wording and personalize the messages or posts. If you want to share your blog post with several different groups, simply add a caption that is relevant to the place you are posting it on Facebook, so it is seen

as a unique post. I would also spread them out over time to be safe.

11. **Watch for competitor saboteurs.** Unfortunately, since it is so easy for people to mark a post, Page, or message as spam, unethical competitors may simply be trolling you or your team's pages and posts and marking them as spam, whether they are spam or not. If you are aware that some-one might be doing this, the first step would be to ban them from your profile or page. This way they will not be able to see your posts or interact with your pages. You can also vis-it their personal Timeline and click the little gear and then Report/Block them individually. Then I would use one of the contact links found on our Resource Page under this chapter to appeal to Facebook and explain what you think has happened.

12. **Some applications that violate Facebook's terms can flag your account or get your Page taken down.** Although most third party Facebook applications are compliant and ap-proved for use by Facebook, some have aspects that are problematic or become problematic over time. App devel-opers have their own sets of rules and procedures to follow and unfortunately some stretch them, sometimes unknow-ingly. Be aware when using an outside application that these can be risky. If you find your account restricted in some way and you were using an outside tool to post or add functionality to your Facebook, check with the app de-veloper to make sure they are in compliance.

13. **Only tag people in posts they appear in and which they would approve.** Never tag someone that is not actually in the picture you are posting, and never when you aren't

100% sure they would appreciate it. Everyone gets a notifi-cation when they are tagged, and if the person removes the tag and then reports the tag, you are at risk. If you want to alert someone to a post, tag them within the comments, don't tag them in the picture when they aren't actually in it.

14. **Only use images you are 100% certain you have permis-sion to use.** You cannot grab an image off the Internet and use it in any way unless it has an open Creative Commons license or you have purchased a license, or you have per-mission from the originator. This includes whether or not you have altered the image or included it in a collage or "Polyvore" style post (those aren't for commercial re-use), or even if you got it from someone else and assumed *they* had permission. It's your responsibility to be sure. The per-son who created the image can very easily do a "reverse image search" to find all the places the image appears, and mark your post as an intellectual property violation, which Facebook takes very seriously. They may even take further legal action. It's not worth it. See my chapter on Avoiding Litigation When Posting Images (page 113).

15. **Do not copy and paste someone else's post or image in order to repost.** Facebook sees this as duplicate content, which poses a similar issue to how Google does not want exact copies of the same blog post or article—it does not serve its readers to have multiple copies, unable to credit the original. It is best to simply click "share" and then add your own content. If you see something you want to say that is similar to someone else's post, create your own ver-biage so it is different. Posts that are repeatedly copied and pasted get flagged as spam or removed from Facebook completely.

I've compiled some articles and resources to help you learn more about handling this issue. Be sure to visit our Resources Page for more information.

Facebook can be a battleground for anyone in the direct selling market. I learned over the last couple of years to follow Facebook rules at all times because, for me, I run my business about 75% on Facebook! One wrong move and all your hard work can be taken away. So know the rules and/or policies both on Facebook and for your business.

Heather Aichele,
Independent Direct Selling Consultant
facebook.com/heather.aichele.14

Do Not Like Each Others' Facebook Pages

I have noticed that direct selling distributors will like the Facebook Business Pages of other consultants or distributors within their own companies. Sometimes they do this because they want to be supportive of their friends, or someone on their team, and sometimes they all agree to like each others' pages in order to help boost the number of likes, thinking that will help increase visibility. Doing this actually has the opposite effect and causes some other problems as well. Here's why:

- When you have "likes" that don't actually interact with your page on a regular basis, Facebook sees them as "ghost" likes, or even fake likes. It throws off the proportion of people who like your page, and people who engage with your page. For example if you have 100 likes but only one person ever comments or likes your posts, it looks suspicious. This is also a reason to avoid "like ladders" that are popular in some direct selling circles.

- Lately Facebook has been showing, on average, that only 2.6% of Business Page posts get to people who like the page. Therefore, the more people who have liked your page who actually want to see your posts, and who could possibly do business with you, and the fewer who aren't truly interested, the better.

- What good does it do to have a lot of likes on your page but none of them buying, booking or joining? Think of an independently-owned franchise store, such as a frozen yogurt shop. Would the owner invite the other fro-yo owners to come into his shop and hang out? And would he or she encourage them to talk about how they love fro-yo, too, especially while wearing the logowear of their own shop? So, yes, the shop may be full of "customers" but they aren't doing any good, and could be doing some damage. This just makes no sense.

- If an individual does by chance like and comment on other distributors' Facebook pages, because pages are public, a "story" goes out to their Facebook friends telling them you liked or commented on that post, and gives them a preview of what that post was about, where they can also visit it and like and comment on it. This confuses our customers when the page you liked or commented on belongs to another representative from the same company. Sometimes, if they aren't familiar with how direct selling works, or are new to the products or your company and you haven't had the chance to build up loyalty, the original distributor could even lose that customer to other distributor.

- Ideally, you, as an independent are branding yourself and your business, creating a kind of business persona that expresses your personal taste, attitude and spin on things. This will help you create a community of people who truly like you and are "fans" of you as a business person versus only being a fan of your product. This is what separates an individual's Business Page from the company's page or other consultants' pages.

But when one person exposes their network to other pages in the company, what if they like those posts better? What if that consultant has done a better job of being creative and compelling in their social media posts? Again, our customers do not always understand how things work and they can either jump ship or inadvertently order, book, or join someone else's team. Or worse, they call the company home office, and when they are asked how they heard about the company, they don't recall. It is important that you establish yourself as their personal consultant—someone who serves their needs, answers their questions, and brings them information they can use. When you share other reps' information, it muddies the water. And yes I have an "abundance mentality" and believe there is plenty of business for everyone, but why make it difficult?

- There is a chance that other consultants will be so passionate about the product that if they DO comment on your posts, it can come across as inauthentic or "pushy." I have seen this happen on corporate Facebook pages as well. The home office will post something about a product and all the consultants will chime in with how amazing the product is. It becomes obvious quickly that the comments are not from customers but from others who have a monetary interest in promoting the product line. Yes, you love the product! But non-reps see the overly promotional comments as spammy. Tone it down, and focus on creating value and adding compelling content to your own Facebook page.

- Liking someone's page because they like you back is not a good strategy. Building up your numbers artificially always backfires in terms of reach and engagement. Be patient and grow your following organically. Post compelling content, interact on a regular basis and provide value. You will have a much more engaged community!

There *is* a better way—adding other distributors to a Facebook Interest List and then checking in periodically. Here's how:

How to Add Pages (and Profiles!)
to Interest Lists on Facebook

- Go to the left sidebar of your Home page and click More next to Interests—then Add Interests to start a new list, and search for Business Pages to add to it.

- You can also do the above for personal Timelines or Profiles as well.

- Give your list a name and decide whether you want it to be public, where anyone on Facebook can see it and subscribe to it, or Friends Only, where your Facebook friends can see it and subscribe to it (both probably not a good idea in this case!) or Only Me where you are the only one who can see it.

- Once added to an Interest List, simply visit your Home page and look under Interests on the left to find your list and click on it. The news feed will then become posts only by people or pages on that list.

- Note that while you are in the Add Interests area, you are given the opportunity to follow, or subscribe to others' public Interest Lists. This can be an additional way to find interesting Pages or Profiles that might be in your target market.

A mistake I see too often is an over obsession on the number of Likes (Fans) a page has. You should be focused on the quality of the likes, not the quantity. The more unengaged fans you have in relation to qualified, engaged fans, the more invisible your page will be in the news feeds of your followers. Low quality fans range anywhere from fake likes to fellow consultants to friends/family who liked your page for support but are not your target market. Here are three things that can help cut down on the number of unengaged fans you have:

1) STOP participating in Like Ladders and Like Exchanges, or asking your friends to like your new Business Page when they are clearly not your target market. This is a big contributor to declining organic reach. It's literally making pages invisible. A person with a real estate business in Dallas has no business liking a page about car repair in San Francisco and vice versa, unless that realtor has a vehicle in SF that needs fixing or the mechanic is looking to buy a home in Dallas. Don't ask other business owners who are not your target market, to come like your page as part of a Like Exchange (like my page and I'll like yours back). The only people who should be liking your page are those you service. If you are going to participate in any kind of Like Exchange program, be very selective about who you ask to like your page. And as a courtesy, don't like pages just to get a Like back. Like them because you actually like the content they provide, and then be sure to engage so you will see more. Cutting back on non-quality Likes and focusing on quality Likes will vastly improve your visibility. If you feel you may have some low-quality Fans that are decreasing your visibility, I would advise removing those Likes.

2) *Do not offer incentives for non-quality Likes that have nothing to do with the type of content your page provides. If you sell hand-made soaps, don't create a contest giving away an Amazon gift card. Yes, everyone could use an Amazon gift card, but "everyone" is not your target market. Offer them a discount on your soaps or a down-loadable tutorial on how to make their own. You can later up-sell them on a course or soap-making kit (if that is something you sell). Offering incentives in exchange for Likes that have nothing to do with your products or services is hurting your reach. This is why I was so happy when Facebook finally did away with Like Gates!*

3) *Never buy Likes! Fake Likes are even worse than the Likes you get from Ladders and Exchanges. These come with their own host of problems, in addition to making you more invisible. Facebook's algo-rithm can detect Likes from fake Facebook accounts and penalize your organic reach for having them, especially if they leave spammy com-ments on your page. Unfortunately, you can still end up with fake Likes even if you never purchased them. These people who like pages for money create fake profiles and like random pages (that they are not paid to like) in an attempt to look more real and try to stay under the radar on Facebook. If a Like looks suspicious, you can delete it.*

Monica Ramos,
Brain Coach and Social Media Trainer
facebook.com/monicaramostv

Avoiding Litigation When Posting Images

There is no denying it, sharing pictures on social media is where it is at. It is what the youth are gravitating to, and it is what adults spend the most time enjoying on social media. It has been said that entrepreneurs who can master visual media will find themselves ahead of others who can't. This is true. It is already happening. Photographs get more response because they make your online business presence more interesting and human. When your social media posts get greater response (likes, comments, shares) you rise to the top.

With this trend though, comes risk. Copyright infringement. And today, especially as a direct seller or top leader, it is critical to play by the rules, respect intellectual property law, copyrights and trademarks, and set the best example for those who follow you. Often people think that because they found an image on the web that it is in the "public domain" and can be shared at will. This is not true, especially for commercial purposes. The original creator and publisher of each item on the web owns its copyright and you may not repost without permission.

I am not an attorney but I have read enough articles by experts to know that intellectual property laws are being broken every second online. And as awareness grows, lawsuits will become more prevalent. I heard recently of one company who was sued for 30 counts of violating copyright by using photos from an actual photo directory site. They thought that by simply linking back to the original post that they would be covered. Not true. In the terms of the site it stated that the site was a gallery site, and the photos were not to be used for commercial purposes. Oops!

One of the best suggestions I've seen is to take your own pictures, or to hire a photographer to take your own custom stock photos. It is something to consider, for sure.

A Note About Polyvore-Style Image Collages

There has been a trend recently of people creating photo collages of different elements of an outfit and adding an image of their product—a purse, clothing, jewelry, nails, and then using that collage image in social media. As if to say, "Look at this great outfit we put together. Our product looks great with it!" These images can be effective for really painting a picture for your prospect when you have a clothing or accessories product that you are marketing.

This particular type of collage has been inspired by the popular shopping site, **_Polyvore.com,_** and sometimes people simply create a set of clothing and accessories on Polyvore itself, take a screen shot, and upload that as their social media post. Both of these social media tactics are problematic.

If you decide to create your own "Polyvore-style" images, you MUST get permission from the original owners of each and every one of the images used in the set, just like any other image used on the Internet, and follow their attribution policies.

You cannot go grab a picture of a dress, and grab a picture of shoes, and throw in a picture of your product and post that collage anywhere unless you have purchased or otherwise secured the rights to use each of those images for commercial purposes.

If you are taking screen shots of Polyvore sets and uploading them as a marketing image on social media you are violating copyright law and Polyvore's terms. The only way you can use Polyvore boards for commercial reasons is to have an agreement with Polyvore, and use their embed code which links back to Polyvore and makes all of the items clickable to the vendors they come from. You can't screen shot it and use as you wish any more than you can screen shot or upload any other picture you find on the Internet. Those images are someone else's intellectual property and copyright. Read Polyvore's terms here (under Redistribution) for starters:
polyvore.com/cgi/terms-of-service

The Bottom Line

You do not have a right to use someone else's picture (even if it is a big brand who "won't notice or care" and/or a small one and you think you are "doing them a favor!") without legal permission in anything you do. It seems every week I hear from someone else who is getting served a cease and desist letter for using images illegally.

I understand how cool it is. I like them, too, and it does help me, as a consumer, make a buying decision when I see them. They are fun to put together. It's a great way to show your style. But it's still not okay to do without permission and because of that, you are putting yourself and your business at risk. Many marketers, brands and photographers use reverse-image searches to find people using their images without permission and you won't have a leg to stand on if you're caught. It's not worth it.

What is the alternative? As I outlined above, purchase royalty free images from some of the stock photography sites. Take your own photographs using your own clothing and accessories. Request permission from vendors to use their photos, perhaps in exchange for including their link. There are ways to do this and keep it legal.

This is an important topic—don't put your business or your company at risk, or steer your team members wrong by using images that are not yours to use. Read the restrictions and requirements on each site where images are available to use or edit, and have fun adding visual flair to your social media content!

On our Resource Page *(smdsbook.com/resources)*, there are some articles to help you navigate the risks, rights and responsibilities of using images in social media. I also have a list of resources to help you use images legally that will avoid litigation for you or even your company who may be held liable for your behavior as a representative for them.

After I complete a blog I like to use some words within my blog to create my image quote. After I pick an image from my image sources I get busy creating my image quote. After my blog is finished I like to place my created image quote at the top of blog, after the title. Yes, this does take time, but I really like to be creative. I have had many comments on blogs and my creative image quotes.

Cora Belle Marburger,

Your Ace Virtual Assistant

facebook.com/YourAceVirtualAssistant

Sharing the Business Opportunity

In social media as well as in "real life" trust is everything, so it is important to provide value and build relationships first and foremost. Here are some ethical and effective ways to attract the right people to your business, and build curiosity about your opportunity.

1. **Be conversational, casual, genuine and friendly**. People join direct selling for people and community more than they join for the specific product or income. When you are posting online, be the kind of person others would want to be around, follow and emulate. If you are too formal, cold, pompous or unengaged, people will not want to be like you. For example, "I'm going to our team meeting tonight. Bringing chocolate-chip cookies! Anyone want to come with?" This tells people you have support (or give it if you are the leader) and that it is fun! Adding emoji makes it even more casual and almost implies you are joking about inviting people, and it makes it easier for people to respond. The right ones will actually message you to say, "Bring me!"

2. **The best results occur when others ask YOU about your opportunity.** Interact in groups and on other pages that discuss business. Without being spammy, when appropriate, mention that you have a business. For example, someone is discussing a restaurant in the local area. You could say that would be a great place for me to meet my clients. Wait for someone to ask you what business you are in, or they might simply visit your Profile to see. Be sure your business info is in your About section.

3. **Share about the lifestyle that having a home-based business affords you.** Stating that you are grateful to have a flexible schedule that allows you to help at your son's classroom party plants the seed in others who would like that flexibility, too. Don't end the status with a link to your business opportunity! You are just sharing from the heart.

4. **Share articles, blogs, and images that support working from home, running a home office, or direct selling in general.** It is best to avoid hype-y sites that make income claims or promise to "change your life." I am not talking about those. I am talking about articles that say how much the direct selling industry contributes to our economy, or that give you tips on organizing your desk, or on the tax benefits of a home-based business. Teach them something they might not know about working from home so they start to realize it would be a great choice for them, too.

5. **Just like in the offline world, putting yourself in the position to meet a lot of people makes a difference.** Hypothetically, if one out of every ten people you meet might be curious about your business, and one out of ten of *those* people might actually request information, and one

out of ten of *those* people actually join, you need to meet a lot of people! In social media, this is best done through interacting in topic discussion groups on Facebook and LinkedIn (not groups where everyone is just sharing their opportunity), by participating in hashtags on Twitter and Instagram, and on other (non-competing) pages on Facebook. Comment authentically and add genuine value to the discussions. You will attract people who will want to find out what you do, and will want to connect to you. Again, be sure your About section is complete!

6. **Offer some kind of "freebie" online in exchange for people signing up on your email list.** Most of you have some mechanism by which you can add people to your company newsletter, or maybe you have created an e-zine on your own. Once people are on your newsletter list, they will be presented on a regular basis with information about your products and opportunity. Come up with a tip sheet you can offer about your topic. This is the "freebie." Create it in MSWord and save it as a PDF. Use a tool such as Google Forms to create a contact form where people give you their name and email address and maybe check off a box about what they are interested in: product, hosting, or joining your team. Announce your freebie on social media and direct them to the contact form link. When you receive their information, email them the freebie. Be sure your freebie is something of value that people benefit from, whether or not they do business with you. They may not be ready (if ever), and you want to be sure to give first.

7. **Images are very powerful in social media today**. Share pictures of you doing business, or pictures of people at your parties or meetings. These grab people's attention and in-

terest them in finding out more. Try using some of the tools at image editing sites such as *picmonkey.com* or *canva.com*. Instagram is a great place to share pictures like this, and you can have them sent to your Facebook and Twitter accounts at the same time. When you share the picture, provide a link to where they can sign up, but be sure NOT to add a call to action on every post. The idea is to create curiosity and intrigue—let them ask you for more information. Once in a while it's okay to purely promote, but keep it to the minimum!

8. **Use private messages or chat wisely.** Do not pounce on someone who displays "green flags" by immediately private messaging them to ask if they would like business information. There is nothing worse for your own reputation, or the reputation of the company or industry as a whole, than to spam people—and pursuing someone too aggressively via private messaging is considered spam. When you do see "green flags" online, indicating someone might be interested, take it as a sign to develop that relationship further and pay attention to them. Perhaps you could interact a little more with them on their own social media profiles (not too much—don't cross over into stalker territory!), which builds rapport. At some point when you feel it would be appropriate to take it to the next level, then private message them or start a chat conversion. It is important to have that rapport FIRST. Once you do, ask permission to go further. "Would you be open to hearing about…?" and "I think what I am doing might help you. Do you want to know more?"

9. **Direct promoting of your business opportunity is okay once in a while.** I recommend my 9-1-1 Code, which con-

sists of nine non-marketing posts (inform, inspire, educate) to every one promotional post (blatant selling/recruiting) and adding in one casual or personal post to build rapport. If you are mostly using subtle engagement and relationship building tactics, providing value and piquing curiosity, then your one promotional post can pack a lot of punch. This is because the rest of the time your followers have come to trust you! When you are ready to do some blatant recruiting, still think of how you can be conversational and social, in doing so. Here are some ideas for posts: you are looking for a certain type of person to round out your team, or your company is looking for reps in certain states. Let them know (if it's true!) that you can't serve everyone and need some help. Talk about your own story and tell them you can help them do the same thing. On promotional posts, I recommend asking people to private message you for more information so you can carry on a conversation, get their contact information or send them information such as a sponsoring video or other materials. If you simply post the link to your business info, it's too easy for people to mentally say yes or no without further discussion. It is kind of like handing them a business card — the sponsoring conversation stops.

10. **Follow up!** Keep in touch with anyone who has been curious about your business. Connect with them on social media and if they've agreed, add them to your newsletter. Check in once in a while via private message to give them the latest information or article that can help them decide if your opportunity is right for them. As you know, in real life, decisions to join your business can take months or even

years. Social media gives you a way to stay top of mind among your prospects if you use it wisely!

BONUS TIP: Do you ever play the "Ask me about my job!" game at home parties? You can do this online, too. I recommend finding (or creating) an image for this type of post and then including the rules in the caption. This engages people even if there is a lot of text to read, and images are more likely to be seen. To follow Facebook's contest guidelines you MUST include something like "This promotion is in no way sponsored, endorsed or administered by, or associated with Facebook." Be clear and concise in your rules. "Ask me about my job! Win a FREE abc by simply asking me about my xyz business! Here's how to win: 1) Like this post. 2) Comment on this post with a question related to my business. One question per person. You need to do these two things to be eligible. The winner will be selected on 123 date and announced on this post. This promotion is in no way sponsored, endorsed or administered by, or associated with Facebook." Find the latest version of Facebook's contest rules on *smdsbook.com/resources*.

Social media has opened up the direct selling opportunity beyond our neighbors. It is so easy to connect through social media and some of your best connections can be with people who you may never meet in person. I have many years of direct selling experience, but I am with a brand new company and social media is making sharing the opportunity so easy. In the first four months, my organization has grown to 139 team members. We have teams everywhere from AK to NY. Social media is a game changer.
Jill Gannon,
Plunder Designs, Independent Stylist
facebook.com/myvintagebling

Social Media Do's and Don'ts

It seems as more people join social media platforms, the lines between personal and business are being blurred. For some people, connections with friends and family are the only reason they are here. For others, promoting their business is their main reason. And still others combine the two, and sometimes those two worlds collide. I've put together a list of Do's and Don'ts for both personal and business that will help. It is not an exhaustive list—every day I find something new I could add. But it's a start!

Do: Invite people to Facebook groups by providing the URL to the group or by having them search for the group name. This allows them the option of joining if they wish.

Don't: Use the built in "Add Member" or "Invite by Email" choices within Facebook groups. These automatically add the person without giving them the choice to opt-in on their own. They will receive posts and notifications immediately and may mark you and the group as spam.

Do: Understand that your Profile is your "home" and you are welcoming others into your space.

Don't: Treat others differently than if they were in your real home. Use the golden rule! Don't type anything that you would not speak out loud.

Do: Comment on your own posts after they've begun to get comments. Add some value, make a relevant or useful comment, acknowledge someone, be social. Not only does this tell your network that you are interactive and social, but it also helps boost your post's visibility as it will pop up in the "ticker" and possibly increase your ranking in the News Feed algorithm.

Don't: Like your own posts. This appears desperate and is redundant. We already know you like the content you are sharing. Liking your own post is like high-fiving yourself in the middle of a conversation with someone, to give yourself credit for something brilliant you just said. It's a little rude. If you want to be funny, add a funny comment, but don't click the like button.

Do: Post a status update regularly—at minimum once a week, or people will think you've quit, or worse. Not posting an update is like never answering your phone. People like to check in and see what you're up to!

Don't: Post status updates ten+ times a day unless you're on Twitter. Your update is like a check-in call. We don't need to know a play-by-play of your day, just as you would not call up your best friends ten times a day on the phone.

Do: Mix business and pleasure. Just as you are a whole person in real life, be a whole person on your social media accounts. Even if your goal is to promote your business, let your visitors in on your non-business side. This will build rapport.

Don't: Go overboard on either business or personal information. Remember that your social media content is timeless, permanent and accessible to a wide net of people, whether you know them now or not. Someone you meet in the future can go back and read your past updates and see your photos. Do not post anything in any format on social media that you would not want broadcast on the evening news.

Do: Be helpful and relevant. Post links, photos and videos that will enhance someone's personal or business life in some way. Just as you'd call up a friend when you read an article about something they'd be interested in, when you find something worthwhile on the web, post it to your Profile or add it to your queue for things to post. You never know whose life you will touch at just the right time.

Don't: Post spammy, controversial or inappropriate links, photos or videos to your social media accounts without realizing the act of posting them is a reflection on who you are. Remember that your Profile is your "home" and imagine these things decorating your walls.

Do: Click the little V at the top right of a post within a Facebook group that you want to be sure to follow and get notifications for. When you click the V, or "down" arrow, you will have the option to "Turn on Notifications" for that post. From that point forward, when more people comment on the post, you will get a red flag notification to alert you. This is useful when a topic comes up in a group for which you would like to learn along with the original poster, but you don't have a meaningful comment to add to that particular post.

Don't: Simply type an asterisk (*) or the word "following" or a period, or other meaningless thing, in order to trigger notifications. Since there is already a "Turn on Notifications" option, use that. When you type an asterisk or other symbol, it produces a notification for everyone involved in that post and they may be excited to read a new comment for more information, only to be disappointed to find nothing.

Do: Send an authentic and personalized welcome message privately to your new friends when appropriate. If you don't know each other in "real life," it is courteous to also mention how you found them, or what or who the connection is that led you to them, just as you would if you went to visit someone in their home. Imagine knocking on someone's door that you would like to get to know, what would you say? Be sincere and authentic.

Don't: Welcome someone whom you have never met by writing on their wall or private messaging them with business information or links. This does not make a good first impression! Let them get to know you over time on their own terms by visiting your Profile when they are interested, where they can read your updates. If you feel you have a product or service that will help them in particular, let them know why, then ask if they'd like more information, and take it to private messages only when the invitation to learn more is clear.

Do: Remember that everyone is watching. Not only your own friends, but your friends' friends, and some you may not even be connected to, depending on your settings. When a friend comments to another friend, their friends can usually read the dialogue as well. Check the privacy settings if you'd prefer only your friends see your activities, but remember you can only control your own privacy settings. Your friends control theirs, so comments or posts on their profiles may be more public than you realize.

Don't: Post links, photos or videos to other people's accounts unless it is relevant and wanted. Would you go to a friend's house and decorate their walls with things you are excited about? Save the decorating for your own Profile, and they can check it out there.

Do: Keep private conversations private. Using comments on a status update to make arrangements for ballet class carpooling by posting back and forth on your wall is a good example. That is something that should be taken to private messages, or chat, or good old fashioned email or telephone. Remember that everyone else is reading what you are posting. If a friend starts a personal conversation in public, divert it by saying you'll private message/email/call them. Not sure? Ask yourself if others will benefit or get to know you better from reading about this.

Don't: Engage in conversations that reference private matters, or give personal details you do not want public. Things like the year you were born, which school your kids go to, that your home will be unattended for a week, are all things that, depending on both parties' privacy settings, can potentially be seen by strangers. If a friend inadvertently reveals too much about you, ask them to delete the public comment and take it private.

Do: Look around! Posted items, status updates, groups and information that people post on their profiles are done so as an expression of themselves and what they are all about. Take the time to click on the various tabs and look beyond their wall or status updates. Get to know them, you might find that you have even more in common!

Don't: Overdo it. Commenting on every update, every posted item, and every photo that someone posts is overkill. Imagine being at someone's home. Would you comment about every single thing, or would you comment on the things that are most relevant or that you are most excited about?

Do: Interact! In "social media," the operative word is "social!" Make comments, add to the conversation, or just let people know you visited. Never participating in two-way conversations makes you a "lurker" and defeats the purpose of being there — to connect!

Don't: Isolate yourself. This is not the place for a monologue . If you want to simply grace us with your presence and wisdom, start a blog and turn off the comments. There is a time and place for that, but social media isn't it.

Do: Integrate your social media sites and feel free to tweet your pins, share your LinkedIn posts to Twitter, and post your Instagram pictures to Facebook, and so on. Chances are your audiences are different on each platform so it is okay to cross-post once in a while.

Don't: Have your Tweets feed into your Facebook Profile or Business Page. There are usually too many of them, too often, and tweets use too much Twitter lingo—it's annoying. Disconnect the auto-publish to Facebook. Sending your Facebook posts to Twitter is perfectly acceptable, though—Just not the other way around.

Do: Invite your friends or followers to tag themselves in your photos. Better yet, when you take a picture you plan to post on social media, ask everyone if it's okay with them, and then tag them. Tagging helps you gain visibility among the other people's networks since the tagged picture shows up on their accounts. You can even have your audience tag their friends in the comments if they'd like to make sure their friends see your post, which can be fun, too.

Don't: Tag people who aren't actually in the picture, note or video. That's "tag spam." If you want to draw attention to someone in particular, you can tag them in a comment.

Do: Feel free to play Facebook games if you like to. They're fun and interactive and you can often meet people and make friends via the chat features.

Don't: Authorize your game apps to post to your Facebook timeline (and therefore OUR news feeds) every time you score, win, "kill" someone in Mafia Wars or need help. If you must share, post manually, not automatically.

Do: Reach out with personal requests once in a while. When you are going through something where you need support, it is okay to ask for it. Be specific and let us in on what you need and why. Don't assume we know or have read all of your previous updates because we may not have seen them.

Don't: Post something dramatic, leaving out crucial information—such as "Oh my gosh I can't believe it!"—without giving the details. This is called "vague-booking." Don't make us beg for information. It's annoying and manipulative. If you don't want to tell the details, don't post about it. If you do want to tell, then tell!

Do: Use Facebook Events to increase attendance at offline events or to promote short term happenings offline or online. Events are a great way to create community among attendees and post information about your event before, during and after.

Don't: Use Facebook Events as a way to promote a non-event such as running a special offer via an Event for a month. This is not an "event" where you require RSVPs and plan to do something at a set time. This is event spam.

Do: Post uplifting and inspiring thoughts, quotes or stories when you feel compelled to. People love to be inspired!

Don't: Share repeatedly negative posts—whining, ranting, venting, complaining about how bad your life is. How is this adding to anyone's life?

Do: Use the "Share" link to share someone's post, or give them a shout out when posting their idea such as, "Thanks to Susie Q for this great tip," for example.

Don't: Repost something original and brilliant another person said without asking permission and/or giving them credit for it.

Do: Feel free to seek advice from your network about business and personal dilemmas or situations. Great conversations and new perspectives can come out of such posts.

Don't: Put your personal problems out there on social media and then get upset when people jump in with advice or offer their opinion. If you don't want a discussion, don't bring it up.

I first met Karen Clark at my company's National Conference and fell in love with her ideas. I try to catch her webinars, which always have great information.

I was able to work all these tips into how I have changed my Facebook postings. Our most recent set of webinars was great. I learned how to change my audience and what is a great time to post to make sure to capture the audience at the high times, and how to schedule posts. Best of all was the Dos and Don'ts of Facebook—in other words, how to stay out of Facebook Jail.

Thank you, Karen, for all the tips!
Tina VanTil, Partylite,
Independent Consultant
facebook.com/tinascandles

Social Media Parties

Social Media Parties Pros & Cons

Have you tried doing online parties for your business? In my personal direct selling career I tried many versions of virtual shows with varied success, so I have been slow to truly endorse online parties as a viable way to do direct sales. I believe there is a time and place for them but in my own experience, and in working for various companies in the industry I would caution any consultant from relying on them as the sole way to do business. Among others who teach social media and Internet marketing in this space, you will find many who are saying that the in-home party experience is dead, and that online shows, Facebook parties, and other social media events are the "future" of this profession. Although I do see their value, I disagree.

It is EASY to generate excitement about an online or Facebook party because of the viral nature of social media. When a consultant posts something about their party, others see it and may even like or comment on things. Any time you post about a product, your network and your attendees' networks might see it. So it "seems" like these are very active and successful! If you are friends with other direct selling consultants, you may even be invited to online parties, and that further reinforces that "everyone is doing it," so it must work, right?

The reality is that for as many people where online shows are great, there are just as many or more people for whom online parties are not working. You do not hear about this because the truth is, no one wants to go online and talk about how something bombed!

When you have a traditional home party business that results in $500-$1000 or more in sales per party, why would you settle for a Facebook party that results in $100-$250 in sales and requires twice as much (or more) time from both you and the host? Yes, there is a place for stand-alone online parties. I know someone who had a successful traditional home party business and was suddenly bedridden. She is doing online parties to keep a trickle of sales going so she can continue to get team bonuses. I know someone else who lives in the hills in West Virginia where it is very difficult to meet people and network enough to get and keep a party chain going. She has turned to online parties as a way to keep up her sales enough to receive a discount for her own use. Online parties can be a great way to give someone who lives far away the experience of your product or ability to earn some for free. They can also help you introduce your company to geographical areas where people may not otherwise ever meet a representative. In these cases, social media parties are a great solution. In the next chapters I outline some options for doing online parties if you choose to. But for most people, the in-home party, if their circumstances allow, is the best use of their time hour for hour.

I believe that for most people, and for most companies, nothing will ever be able to replicate the experience of seeing and speaking with people in person, demonstrating products face to face with the chance for customers to get their hands on your product, see its quality and to see your eyes light up when you describe what the business opportunity has done for your family. Nothing online can compare to a group of people sitting around talking about what they are buying, and passing around their favorite products or samples.

As a consultant, at an in-home experience you are able to read the non-verbal cues of your guests, see their eyes light up when you talk about your product or opportunity, and have a better sense of who might be interested in booking the next party or joining your team. In-person gatherings allow the consultant to connect heart to heart with her host and guests in a way that builds loyal relationships more easily than online. Social media parties can give people an experience of your company, but it just isn't the same and I will continue to say this despite being in the minority.

Direct selling companies, where the majority of their representatives do online parties, and for some companies that started as "online only" opportunities, are now, after some time has passed, finding sales and sponsoring declining. You can see that they are creating home party programs or beefing up their host rewards in order to attract more in-home experiences so that they can balance their businesses. What they have found is that while convenient and effective in the short term, businesses that are 100% online don't lend themselves to one of the best benefits of using the direct sales model — duplicability.

When companies or leaders provide systems that are easy to duplicate regardless of experience or skill, those teams thrive long-term because success really is achievable for everyone. By relying too heavily on technology, you are dealing with so many variables among prospects and new consultants: comfort level with technology in general, the existing network size of the consultant and her customers, hosts and their comfort level with technology, or simply whether someone has an innate "tech savvy" personality or not. If a leader has a great propensity for online marketing and every person she sponsors onto her team is just like her, great! That is rare. If we all were able to add people to our teams who were just like us, every person would be successful every month. The reality is that you will attract a variety of folks and need to have options.

There is definitely a need to serve customers at a distance and thus an online party solution may be necessary as a supplement—but not necessarily a replacement—for traditional home parties. Given the limitations of the technology thus far, and the relatively lackluster results and lack of duplicability for many people compared to live demonstrations, it doesn't make sense for most consultants to place a priority on online parties. However, if you do find that you would like to supplement your business with online parties, ask yourself these questions:

1. **Do we have enough of a contact base to work with (you or a host)?** Traditional home party training suggests inviting 4x as many as you expect to attend a live party. Online this is true, and then some. Only count contacts who are personally connected to you, know you and trust you—not random Facebook friends who have never interacted with you. Be prepared to personally invite each person, or to coach your host to do so.

2. **What is my goal for the online party?** Expect on average half the sales, bookings and sponsoring you might find in traditional home parties. This is a normal and acceptable standard. It may be that for you and your situation this is fine. The trade-off for being able to truly work from home,

or to be able to serve your long distance customer may be worth it.

3. **Do you have an email newsletter that you can add contacts to**? This will give you a chance to stay in touch long after the online party, especially with those who did not buy/book/sign up. Conversions often happen after the party has closed. When setting up your online party, create a registration form, online drawing slip or other "lead capture" where you can gather all attendees' email addresses for this purpose. Company newsletters can be set up to allow consultants to then manually input or import a spreadsheet of those leads into their monthly newsletter. Or you may choose to use your own email service, such as Mailchimp or another tool if your company allows it.

4. **What do I want to model for my team?** Remember that everything you do is duplicated. If they see you doing a lot of online parties and posting about them frequently, they will naturally assume this is the way to run their businesses as well. This may not be a problem, especially if you are able to train them with some tips for success. However, some consultants will assume they do not need to still make calls or visit people in person and will find themselves struggling to grow their businesses over time.

Great Reasons to Do Online Social Media Parties

- **When you need to pad your volume a little,** have an online show you host yourself if that is allowed in your company. Make it a "mystery host" party and give away host rewards to lucky winners, but make sure your company allows this format. This encourages purchases and participation. I know several consultants who do these on a monthly basis, and it can be a great way to reach your own network and show them what online parties are like.

- **When you are unable to do home shows** due to medical reasons, childcare situations, or transportation challenges. Things happen that prevent some people from getting out and doing parties. Of course, it is better to do online shows than to stop doing business all together, and it can work until you are able to return to working your business more fully.

- **If you have a long distance host or prospect** who really wants a show to earn host rewards but would rather work with you than find someone local to do one for her, offer an online party. An online party will allow you to keep that host in your business where she might otherwise find someone else.

- **When your host has a lot of long distance friends** she would be inviting. Something fun to try is to do a social media party in conjunction with an in-home party, either after or as a follow-up or second party.

- **During severe weather.** In the worst winter months or with inclement weather looming, either plan in advance to conduct virtual shows, or if a show needs to be canceled due to unexpected severe weather, reschedule it as an online show.

- **When you are truly an introvert.** This is less talked about but if the idea of presenting in front of groups or going into someone's home is uncomfortable and you are unwilling to "stretch" your comfort zone yet, then an online party could be a good solution. Online parties allow some introverts to do business more consistently because they may be more comfortable, though I would encourage you, as your confidence builds in your business, to try doing an in-home show now and then for the benefits they provide.

- **If you are in a very rural area** where networking opportunities are sparse and it's a challenge to meet new people on a regular basis, doing more online networking—and then offering to conduct social media parties—can help you keep your business going. You might need to travel a little further but I'd still encourage in-person experiences, too.

- **If you are a single parent or one whose spouse works late/night shifts,** and you have no one to watch the kids while you do parties, doing them online might work. I'd encourage you to get creative with childcare if you can, though. I was a military mom with a spouse who was away a lot. I know the struggle, but I also know that getting out to "work" is fun, too! Try kid-friendly parties in the daytime, swapping kid duty with another consultant, bringing a teen with you, or finding someone you trust to watch your children—maybe even a customer who would trade for product!

- **When you want to do your own party** for something like a new catalog launch, seasonal open house or mystery host party, **but your home or apartment is too small to conduct it in your own place**, an online party is another option. However, parties in creative places like restaurants or parks, or borrowing someone else's home work, too.

As you can see, there are indeed some very good reasons for turning to online social media parties. I am not "against" doing them at all, I just want to make sure you are aware of the pitfalls, as well as the opportunities, in doing them. Besides my own experience doing online parties when I was in the field, I have spent the last two years studying the best way to do online social media parties so that we may increase the success rates and the duplicability of them when consultants choose to do them to supplement their marketing efforts. The following chapters outline some best practices. You can decide for yourself at what level you would like to incorporate these into your business.

I have used Social media, mostly Facebook, to keep customers interested. Several customers of mine have moved away from our area, but continue to host online parties with me. I have used Facebook to meet and network with others and build my team.

I use Facebook events for in-home parties to create a little "pre-party" for every host, which gives me the chance to interact with her guests beforehand. I can help her generate more interest in my product, as well as keep the guests excited, and build a relationship with that person who can't make it last minute. It's helped me stay in touch with customers, meet new ones, and gives me the opportunity to do business (online parties) after work on a night when I am too tired to really want to be doing a live demonstration. I create groups to connect with my team, and I use Pages to stay in touch with my customers.

Mary Bacon,
Independent Consultant for Steeped Tea
facebook.com/steepedteawithmarybacon

Host Coaching for Social Media Parties

Host coaching is critical, especially when you are conducting a virtual show through Facebook, Instagram, Pinterest or any other social media platform where the majority of the activity takes place within that platform. It is vital that you and your host take preparations for the party seriously while also having fun! By that I mean that this is a great time for you to build a relationship with your host that is a combination of friendship and business. As you work with her, she will see how you are professionally, and can learn your systems. If the right amount of rapport and trust is built in the process, you may find that she makes a great new team member, too!

"Your host is your best recruit" is a phrase that is commonly heard in direct selling, and that's because it is true. If you think about it, your host, if she is doing her job the way you've modeled and asked her to, is already "selling" your company, your product and the home or online party marketing avenue to her core group of family and friends. She is likely a lover of your product, and now as a host, she has become an advocate for you. If the relationship building that occurs during host coaching goes well, it is only natural for her to—at the very least— consider doing what you do.

Following are some things to make sure that you do during the very important host coaching phase of holding social media parties:

1. Don't skimp on host coaching. In fact, I would say that it is even more important for an online party than for a home event. If you are the host doing your own online party, go through all the standard host coaching steps with yourself! If you have a host, guide her toward success and emphasize the importance of doing her part—the enjoyment of her guests and her host benefits depend on it.

2. Early on, see what her communication preference is. It may be texting or private messaging, or it may be calling on the phone. Find out her preference and make note of it so you can reliably communicate with her. Whenever you can, go over things on the phone while you are both at the computer, or consider using a screen share or video chat program. Resist the temptation to communicate with your host only through Facebook—sometimes she won't see your messages and host coaching is just too important to rely on only one method of communication. If you're having a hard time reaching her, consider reaching out in another way.

3. Give her a heads up about how the party is going to go, emphasize that it is important that she chime in and that she can make a big difference in her party total by engaging with your posts. Build rapport and encourage her. There's nothing like hearing from you in an enthusiastic and caring way to get her on board with what needs to be done. The

trust and rapport you build with your host will make a big difference!

4. Your host must personally invite everyone. By that I do not mean that she should add each of her guests' names to a mass message or an email. I mean personally invite them, in a way that is personalized to each guest and her situation or her style, or her needs or the way she wants to communicate.

5. Ask how she thinks her friends might like to be contacted and encourage her to think about that as she reaches out to invite them. Here are some tips for the various methods she might try:

    Phone call: If she gets their voicemail, have her leave a message with her excitement shining through and that she will follow up with a private message with the link to the party.

    Texting: Keep it short and sweet, but include the link to the party.

    Email: Have her send single, personalized emails that include the link to the party, not a mass email to multiple people.

    Private message: Again, personalized and unique. Coach her to send these only to her friends she thinks will be interested. Tell her it's very important to make each message unique and not to copy/paste, and not to send these messages too close together in time. This is to prevent the social media site from inadvertently categorizing her posts as spam.

Share the party on her Personal Profile as a general invitation, asking for help spreading the word such as, "Share if you know someone who would be interested, too!"

Mail a postcard or paper invitation: Include the link to the party so her guests can type it in and join in. (A shortened link works great!) You would be surprised at how effective paper mailed invitations work for online parties!

6. Inviting her guests is the most "work" your host will need to do, and although it will take her some time, it is worth it. When one of her guests says that they can attend or are interested, or if they are a "maybe," she can then send them the link to join the party, or she can use the Invite button if one is available—but only if she gets a Yes or a "maybe." We don't want her adding people to the party if they are clearly a "no" or have not responded.

7. Something that works really well is to have her make a list of about 25-50 people she might invite, and then take notes about each person and what would be in it for that particular person to attend and use your product. Have her think of the benefits and features, matching them to each person and their own situation. Or have her consider the pain points that she can touch on when she talks to them. Offer to help with this part if she isn't very familiar with your product line yet.

8. It is far better to have a smaller party where everyone is interested and most likely to interact than to send out mass invitations with poor response, or people who are there but not interacting. Besides, when someone is invited and sees there are 100s of guests, they don't feel very special. This cannot be emphasized enough. It's important for the quality

of the party to have active and engaged guests who really want to be there either to learn about your company or to support their friend. If your host insists she has far more friends who would like to attend, suggest she book another party for the next group of friends.

9. When direct sellers conduct traditional in-home party experiences they will often have their host send them the Yes and Maybe list including contact information, and then the consultant will mail out paper invitations or reminder cards. There is no rule that says you cannot do offline invitations for an online event! In fact they can be very effective in making your host's guests feel wanted and welcome. Doing this also gives you a way to gather the guests' contact information so you can follow up more easily.

10. I recommend that you prepare your posts or images in advance but also be willing to be flexible and customize to your host and her guests. Every gathering is and should be different. Have a conversation with her about the types of friends she is expecting. You can even go over her guest list with her and find out specific things about each one, or have her send you her notes she took before inviting people. For example, if you find out they are mostly moms with little kids, you will want to make sure to mention any family friendly products you carry. If they are mostly women of a certain age, you can gear your presentation to that demographic.

11. Mail or email your host a packet of information about your company, its products and host benefits. Most companies have these materials prepared for in-home parties and they work great for online parties as well. Include samples if

your company has them, so she may experience your product before the party, which will help her enthusiasm since you won't be together in person. If you do not have samples with your company, consider letting her borrow one of your products and then keep it as part of her host rewards if her party reaches a certain level. It is best to send this out at least a week in advance of her party, and encourage her to use her samples as soon as possible so she can speak from experience when telling her friends how great it is! Coach her through using the product so she has a positive experience. Then, ask her to take a picture of her with it so she can post within the party. Having her use the product in advance ensures she will have experience when she makes her invitation calls and can truly speak from the heart about how fun and easy it is and what the quality is like.

New Guidelines for Facebook Parties

The popularity of Facebook parties in particular has been increasing rapidly, and although many consultants have been having luck with them, many others are finding them to be either ineffective, inefficient, or in some cases, a source of trouble with Facebook itself.

What Is a Facebook Party?

A Facebook party is when a direct seller invites their connections, or those of a host, to join them on Facebook "live" for a period of time. She then discusses the products, opportunity and benefits of hosting. During the party, there might be some fun games to generate excitement, and give away prizes. Orders, bookings and sponsoring happen either on the consultant's website, or by private messaging or emails. There are many variations, but they generally follow a similar format, all conducted through posts, usually images, posted onto Facebook.

What Is Going On?

In recent months, many distributors, and entire companies, have been experiencing more and more "Facebook Jail" issues due to Facebook party activities. Facebook Jail is when you are restricted in some way from using Facebook's functions, as described in the How to Avoid "Facebook Jail" chapter on page 99. Here are some of the things I have seen happen:

- Restricted from posting in groups for a certain time

- Suddenly unable to access any events you administer

- Posts being deleted by Facebook

- Images not loading

- Unable to send private messages

- Links leading to a warning about spam

There are a few theories as to why this is happening more lately, especially in relation to online parties. Maybe competitors are reporting Facebook parties as spam. Maybe friends who see the posts, mark them as spam, not understanding why they are seeing them. Some say Facebook does not approve of "work at home schemes" and have grouped the direct selling profession in with known scams and pyramid schemes, not understanding this multi-million dollar legitimate industry.

What Can We Do About This?

As I mentioned in the Social Media Parties Pros & Cons chapter (page 135), I recommend we look at Facebook parties as a supplement, an "extra" the way a vendor fair or catalog party would be. Use online parties for long distance hosts, or as a way to maintain excitement among your own out-of-town connections. When you rely on Facebook too much, you put your entire business at risk because you are at the mercy of Facebook—a business in its own right with its own rules that its representatives are free to interpret and apply in any way they see fit at any time. In reality, we are using their tool, usually for free, to grow our businesses and it is up to us to do what we can to comply with their wishes and avoid Facebook Jail.

The following are ten guidelines for conducting Facebook parties if you choose to continue to hold them. See the next chapter for my specific recommended party how-tos.

1. Facebook wants **all business transactions to occur through a Business Page,** not a Personal Profile, nor groups or events administered through Personal Profiles. It is okay to use groups for support or discussions about your business, or to use Personal Profile events to gather RSVPs and generate excitement for an offline party, but Facebook does not want the "sales" and calls to action to occur anywhere but on a Business Page.

2. **Create an Event from your Business Page.** This means that your Facebook party will be public but we already know that due to Facebook's News Feed algorithm, only a tiny percentage of "likes" on our pages see our posts so this is not as much of a problem as you might think. If you have a host, add her to your event and then make her a co-host, and then she can add her friends to the party after personally inviting them some other way.

3. Facebook events that are created by a Business Page **can be promoted** by paying a small amount to increase exposure if it is a public event, or to make sure a targeted group sees the event posts. Consider budgeting a small amount for this if your company allows you to use paid boosting on Facebook.

4. **Personally invite** guests or coach your host to do so. Email is a great option. Personalized private messages can work. (Do not copy/paste the same message to everyone though!) Share the event link and give guests the option to join vs. adding them yourself. Mail a postcard. Give them a call. Do whatever you can to make sure they are aware of the party, and invite them to opt-in to join. Only add people to the event page yourself if you know they are a Yes or a "maybe." If you have a host, coach her to do the same and to really think about each guest and to personalize the invitation.

5. When it comes to Facebook parties, **less is more.** It is better to have 25 engaged and interested invited guests than 500 who do not want to be there, do not engage with the posts, and do not take action by purchasing, hosting or joining your team. I recommend inviting no more than 50 guests.

6. Consider setting your event up one to two weeks in advance and then **pre-populate the event** with posts and information about your company before ever inviting anyone. Posting more than one image at a time in a mini-album reduces the amount of single posts going out to your "likes." Just be sure to go back and edit the captions of each image to reflect the features and benefits of the product or service you are highlighting.

7. During the first week before your live party, after your party is set up correctly, begin inviting people to the event, as described in Number 4 above. Post no more than once per day on the event page leading up to your live event, to **begin generating excitement.**

8. Set your party up to be **held live during a thirty- to sixty-minute time frame**. The more posts you have that are not engaged with by your guests, the more red flags that go up for Facebook. By conducting your party during a short "live" period, you are more likely to create a sense of urgency among your guests, which will compel them to comment on your posts and take action. The short time frame also keeps it exciting for the guests who may tire of seeing several posts a day as they did in 10- or 14-day style parties.

9. Make sure your images and messaging are in **compliance with your company guidelines and with copyright law**. Do not take an image off of the web and use it or doctor it without permission from the original owner. Facebook takes copyright violations very seriously. Follow your company guidelines for use of logos and images. It is not uncommon for other consultants to "mark as spam" those who are out of compliance.

10. **Keep it simple.** Everything you do in direct selling is potentially duplicated by your team or future team and when you complicate your Facebook party by creating elaborate videos, custom images, or complicated contests, you could be scaring off your prospects. Whenever possible, your Facebook party should mirror your traditional home party format. By creating an online version of your regular party steps, you are setting yourself up for success based on your own company's guidelines, you are more likely to get results, and you are less likely to find yourself in Facebook Jail.

Conducting a Facebook party when used within these guidelines can be a beneficial way to earn more sales and meet more people, on a platform that is ripe for relationship marketing. If you choose to conduct a Facebook party, consider following these tips and the how-to's in the next chapters and you will reap the benefits which result in a win for you, a win for your host, a win for the guests, and of course a win for Facebook!

Facebook Parties How-To

When it comes to social media events, Facebook parties were the first version of online parties to gain popularity and sweep through the direct selling industry. Many of us had been conducting online meetings and parties through other tools such as webinars, live streaming, chat rooms and forums. However, when Facebook became more mainstream, it was obvious that we had to find a way to use it for online shows as an option for parties in those circumstances I described in the Social Media Parties Pros & Cons chapter (page 135). It's where most of the people are!

I'd like to also acknowledge direct selling training specialist, Jennifer Harmon, who helped me fine-tune this system so that it not only works to achieve results for you — the consultants — but also so that it honors corporate and Facebook requirements.

I've enjoyed hearing the success and ease that people are experiencing doing things "my" way. The comments I hear most are that this method frees you from worry about "spam" or "Facebook Jail" and that it is easier and faster with higher party averages. I hope you will find the same!

Here's the way I recommend you do Facebook parties (if you choose to!)

Use an Event Started from Your Facebook Business Page

Facebook is becoming more consistent in enforcing their rules for selling through the Facebook platform and as I have already mentioned, Facebook prefers sales and other business transactions occur through a Business Page, not a Personal Profile, a private event or a group. Facebook groups are still a great way to support your team, to provide an additional service to people who have purchased product, or to create a VIP or Host-Only group that generates a sense of community among your most interested "fans" without selling to them. Groups are an amazing way to offer support and discussion that isn't geared toward completing sales.

An Event that originates from yours or your host's Personal Profile is also still a great way to gather RSVPs for an in-home party in a more private and secure way, without conducting any sales within that event. I love that personal events generate notifications that will remind your guests of the in-home party they RSVP'd to.

However, events originating from your Business Page, with your host as a co-host, are currently the best solutions for live Facebook selling parties. In the previous chapter I explained a bit about this, and in the following chapter you will find some important tips that explain this recommendation. Also see our Resources Page for links to Facebook's terms related to this kind of activity. I know that, in the past, when Facebook parties started, groups and personal events made sense, but they don't any more, so please give this a try! There really are some great benefits and when you do need to conduct an online party, I think you'll find success this way.

1. For one thing, **Business Pages on Facebook are professional** as they come from your business and aren't connected to
   your personal posts. Some people like to friend their customers, but when you have a large, successful customer
   base or team, you might find that you actually want to start
   separating your personal online presence from your business presence on Facebook anyway. Not everyone needs to,
   or even wants to, be your Facebook friend. See my chapter
   on Social Media Do's and Don'ts (page 123) for more cau-
   tions about this.

2. Facebook Business Pages also **include analytics** (called Insights) that you can't get on a Personal Profile, on a personal
   event or in a group. This makes it easy for you to see what
   is benefitting your business and what isn't. You can look at
   page likes, reach, where people are coming from and which
   parts of your page they are visiting. You can look at which
   posts are performing the best, and which time of day people
   most respond. You can even look at more specific de-
   mographics of the people who visit the page.

3. A Facebook event that starts from a Business Page can also
   be **targeted to people in specific locations or de-
   mographics.** In fact, if your company allows it and you
   decide you wanted to invest a little bit to promote your
   event, you can even target your event to an email list that
   you upload. Can you imagine how your response rate
   would improve if you could pay a little money (even $1 or
   $2) to make sure the event posts were visible to your host's
   guest list? This is a great benefit that you can only find on
   events started from a Business Page.

4. And best of all, it is very rare for a Business Page or any activity originating from it to receive any kind of negative restriction or "Facebook Jail" problem that I described in the How to Avoid "Facebook Jail" chapter (page 99), because Business Pages were created **for** business. As long as you are following Facebook's Business Page Terms and Community Guidelines, you are good!

The more people who like your Page and interact with it, the more visibility your business has on Facebook in general. There can be a ripple effect on your general Facebook presence just from the act of conducting an online party on an event through your page.

When conducting a Facebook party or any social media party, simpler is better. As tempting as it is to explain everything about your product, booking rewards and business opportunity, it's easy to overwhelm your guests with too much information, which makes it harder to get them to make a purchase, to book a party, or join your team. Just like in offline parties, your host is your very best prospect! Your host and her guests are curious and watching how you conduct your Facebook party. When you create an elaborate and complicated Facebook party, the chances of your host wanting to do what you do is diminished, as are your bookings. It is important to also create systems your own team can replicate with their own online parties if you want them to find success as well. The less complicated they are, the better for sales, bookings, sponsoring and your own team development.

As you develop your own Facebook parties, keep this in mind: Your goal is to have most informational posts pre-loaded into your event as most people join a few days before the party, and then to have a simple thirty-minute "live" party which is easier for your host and her guests to attend. Keep the party event open a few days after the live portion ends so that you can follow up. The whole process is short and sweet!

Some consultants have found success with longer formats such as a week or ten days and that's fine. In general the format I recommend is easy and duplicable for most consultants. Whichever format you use, mine or something else, the best way to reach your party goals is for you and your host to both engage with the guests as much as possible so that you can begin positioning yourself as their new consultant. With Facebook parties, we don't have the physical interactions and demonstrations like you would at an in-home party, but you can still encourage participation. Interact with the guests, respond to their comments, tag them in comments when appropriate, ask them questions about what they like, or answer the questions they post to you. Encourage your host to do the same — the more they hear from her, the more likely they are to purchase. Just like at an in-home party, they want to support their friend. In direct sales, we know that for offline parties the more you connect with people, the better your results will be. The same is true for online parties, so keep that in mind and plan to be hands-on!

Create a Folder on Your Computer to Store Items

One of the first things you're going to want to do is to prepare your posts in advance by creating a folder on your computer to store items you will need during your Facebook party. In this folder, save any of your own images or your company's images that you might want to use in your party so that they are easily accessible. It's a good idea to name them something that makes it easy for you to pull up particular images later. Some people like to number their party posts but I find it easier long-term to rename the file in a way that is recognizable, such as HostRewards.jpg or WhyStory.mp4 and so on.

If you are tempted to use other images or create your own, always make sure they are in compliance with your company policy as well as general Internet copyright law as I explained in the chapter, Avoiding Litigation When Posting Images that starts on page 113. For those of you who are so inclined, try making a video of your opening talk or introduction. This is a great way to build rapport, just keep it simple and something others can duplicate. Remember that they are watching! Don't worry about using special effects or overly editing your video with fancy software or apps. A simple video shot from your smart phone works well, and is something that others who are thinking about doing your business will find doable.

Save Needed Links and Text

Another thing that's helpful is to set up a text document with the verbiage or links you might need, and save it into this same party folder where you are storing your images. In general, it's not a great idea to copy/paste repeatedly on Facebook but it's okay to copy and paste links as needed, along with the occasional pre-written post. If you do a lot of Facebook parties, I'd recommend making this document more like an outline with notes and creating the verbiage fresh each time, rather than scripting things out exactly. Remember, whenever possible you want to customize your posts to your specific host and her guests, so pre-planning every word isn't really going to work, but having some general ideas is great!

Setting Up Your Business Page Event

If you have not already done this, you might want to turn off the auto-sharing of Facebook events on your main Facebook

Business Page. This will prevent a new post from being generated on your page wall every time you create an event. To do this, go to the Events tab on your page. If it's not visible you might have to go to the "More..." button near your cover image and find it there. If you still can't find it, check your Settings for your Business Page, and then under the Apps section you'll be able to make sure the Events "app" is visible. If you have never created an Event on your Page and do not see the Events tab, create a "test" event to generate it, and then simply delete the test. Once you've clicked on that Events tab, you can click the little gear on the far right. Uncheck "Publish Events to Time-line." This just makes it less likely that you will get non-guests participating — if that is something you are concerned about — since the event is technically public.

Click on Create Event to start. Let's go over what you might put in each section:

1. **Cover Image.** For the Event Photo at the top you can either leave in the one Facebook defaults to, or you can upload something else. There are no restrictions to the types of images you can use here, so you may either put a photo that is related to your business or a general image, perhaps of ladies having fun at a party, or create a graphic of your own. Use a regular Facebook sized cover image similar to the size of the one on your Business Page.

2. **Event Name.** Holly Host's ABC Party!

3. **Details.** This is your event description. Include a brief explanation of what your company is about and how to order. Mention that during the live party they should refresh their Page to see current discussions/posts at the top.

4. **Where.** Right Here on Facebook!

5. **Tickets.** Great opportunity to insert your clickable party link here—the word Tickets will be clickable to anyone reading the party description and lead to your website link or the specific party link.

6. **When.** I recommend setting it up (or at least starting the invites/pre-party part) two to three days or a week out—not too long, but not too short either. Create a sense of urgency. Which day or what time is really up to you. There is no magic formula. In general I've always felt that the best times are what's convenient to you and your host, so that you are both able to be "all in" during your live event!

7. **Category.** Choose the Community category and then Shopping subcategory.

8. **Tags.** This is a way to tell Facebook the topic of your event so that it can suggest it to other people on Facebook. Since you most likely would not want your Facebook parties to be publicized to others, just leave this section blank.

9. **Checkboxes.** Keep the remaining boxes unchecked for "only Hosts being able to post" and for "posts needing to be approved." You can always edit the event to check those off later if you find it necessary.

Next, click Publish at the bottom. I do not recommend using the Save Draft or Schedule option since you will be unable to post to your event or pre-fill it will information until the published date.

You will see that on your Event page there are now two tabs, About and Discussion. When you or your guests visit the

Event, the default view is the About tab so be sure to click the Discussion tab to see all posts and comments on the Event.

Now, visit your Event page and at the top copy the link/url of your Facebook Page Event so you can give it to your host to use in her invitations. If you want, you can use a URL shortener to make that easier (*bitly.com* is good since it is trackable and customizable such as *bitly.com/HollyHostParty*). Add that link to your Facebook party text document so you have it handy, too.

Note: Do not "join" the event yourself. If you do so, it will be as your personal profile, which would trigger posts in the newsfeed of your friends each time you post or comment within the event. This is more problematic for you as the consultant due to the majority of the posts coming from you. Since your Business Page is the original "host" of the event, joining as your personal profile is not necessary.

Set Your Party Up for Success!

In addition to the thirty- to sixty- minute live portion of your Facebook party, it is a good idea to pre-populate your Facebook event with several informational posts, and then you can do several pre-party posts that you start several days before the live event, but after people have joined in. Then you will have the posts during the actual live party, and after that a few follow-up posts. Your host and her guests will have access to you and your information over the course of several days, while also being there LIVE with you during the thirty- to sixty- minute portion of your party. So think about it in terms of having pre-existing information in your event, then daily posts before and after your party, and a live time period of about thirty minutes where you post six to eight posts (and maybe additional information in the comments) for the "party" portion.

Your Schedule Might Look Something Like This:

Two Weeks Prior: Mail your host any samples or loaner product, and the host packet. During the week after she receives it, call her to coach her through using it and what to expect during the Facebook party. Emphasize that it is vital that she play an active role both before the party as well as during the event. You may also want to set up another time to talk and go over her guest list with her, giving her ideas of how to personalize her calls or messages.

Ten Days Prior: Set up your event as described above. Pre-fill your Event page with some of the more informational posts you've saved, adding a brief caption to each image. Make your posts fun and exciting, and add a question if possible, to encourage comments. In this step we are pre-filling the posts before the party starts but people will see them when they RSVP. You want to encourage engagement where you can.

Some types of post you might pre-fill would be:

- About your company/company history

- A how-to or general information about your product line(s)

- Your host rewards or current host special

- A post or two about one of your lesser-known product lines or a great value you offer

- New Consultant Kit image or other business opportunity post.

- Any company-created videos about your company or business opportunity

Pin your favorite post to the top of the Event page (click the little down arrow or "V" next to a post to Pin to Top) so that something interesting is waiting for them at the top when they first visit. The general "About this company" type post or a video works well there. Some people like to pin and unpin posts throughout their events; it is up to you.

Eight Days Prior: Your host starts to personally invite her guests. See the Host Coaching for Social Media Parties chapter (page 143) for suggestions on how she can do that. I do not recommend giving her the link or adding her to the Event page until she at least starts the personal invitations. This will encourage her to talk to her guests a bit about the party, to see whether they are a Yes or a Maybe instead of just adding them without contacting them personally. It is up to you. Some people prefer to get it all out at the same time, but for the best success, I would wait a day or even require that she submit her Yeses and Maybes to you before getting the link. If she is Facebook-savvy, she may figure out that she can find the link herself on your Events tab but I would explain to her the importance of doing things in this order and get some buy-in from her.

Seven Days Prior: When you feel your Event is ready to go, and perhaps you've started to hear that your host is gathering some interest, invite her to the Event page in one of two ways. You can either send her the party event link or use the Invite button if you are her Facebook friend. If you have coached her this far, she should be expecting it, so it's okay to just add her. You can't use the Invite button unless you're Facebook friends, which will be most cases, so simply send her the Facebook party page link.

Once she joins as Going, go back to the Event link and click Edit. Next to where it says host, add your host's name next to your Page name. She has to already have marked that she is Going for this to work. This will make you each co-hosts, and she will be able to easily do the next step. Remember, there is no need to mark yourself as Going to the event. Your Business Page already is attending!

Five Days Prior: Have your host send the link to the party to her Yes and Maybe lists, or she can use the Invite button once she has gotten confirmation from them. It is preferable if they add themselves via the event link, especially if she has not gotten firm commitments. Remember, it is better to have a smaller, more engaged party, than for her to do mass invites to random Facebook friends. This will benefit both of you! It may take her some time to do this part, but it will pay off with host benefits.

As guests start to JOIN the Event Page, begin interacting by commenting on the posts and liking their comments, and answering any questions. Remember, it is very important to engage with the guests and build relationships. Encourage your host to do the same. Be casual and personable, friendly, not formal—be yourself! Respond in the way you would if someone were to speak with you at an in-home party or other setting. You are on duty. Be helpful, cheerful, and enthusiastic about what you're doing. Reading text online makes it challenging to catch the tone of voice or cheerfulness so don't be afraid to exaggerate your reactions a little—add some fun emoji or punctuation or a cute picture or sticker when you comment. This will create that sense of fun that we want to convey, and fun makes it easier to get more bookings!

Three Days Prior: Post a welcome or "roll call" so that those who have arrived can check in. This is a good post on which to do a general door prize drawing after everyone has checked in. You can let them know you'll do a random drawing of all who comment on that post, and announce the winner just as the live party starts, or toward the end—it is up to you. Alternatively, you can post a link to a contact form you may have on your site, or you can create one in Google Forms. Include the link in your roll call post and choose your winner from those entries. A combination of these also works well, such as, "fill out my form here, and comment with where you're from."

Two Days Prior: Post a general introduction as to how the party will work. Have your host comment about how excited she is! Be mindful not to post new items too often within the Event. One new post a day to build excitement is great. Then spend the rest of the time commenting on those and your pre-filled posts to get the guests looking at them or watching the videos. Commenting on existing posts is a great way to add more value and information without adding too many new posts—that can be overwhelming. Ask your host to check in on her Party now and then to respond to comments and interact as well, bringing her own enthusiasm. A simple "I love that about ABC Company!" by her on one of your posts can do wonders to let her friends know she is totally into this!

One Day Prior: Post something about your host and how awesome she is. Invite people to comment how they know her, or a fun fact about her, or some other fun way to recognize your host. The night before the live Facebook party, or the morning of, ask your host to do personal reminders to the guests. Have her call or text those that she has numbers for, email or private message others (remind her to individualize her messages).

Day of the Party: Notifications reminding the guests that there is an event "today" will automatically go out to anyone who has Joined/is Going or marked themselves as Interested on the event. Ask your host to share the Event again to her own personal Facebook Timeline as well, to catch any stragglers who she may not have been able to reach.

Just before the party, unpin the post you might have had "pinned" to the top so that your most recent post will be up there. If you like, you can pin each post as you conduct your live party and ask your guests to refresh the Event page every few minutes—just remember to unpin the last one first—you can only have one pinned at a time!

Post one more reminder on the Event Page fifteen to thirty minutes before the party is to start. This will generate a new notification even though those who RSVP'd will get one from Facebook earlier in the day as well. We have to make it easy for people to remember to show up live!

Party Time! Conduct the thirty- to sixty- minute LIVE portion of the party using the suggestions mentioned above. Post something about every five to ten minutes with a new image, a link, a video or other information. Your goal is to get conversations going, keep people engaged, get sales so your host can be rewarded, book more parties to replace this one—and some to grow on—and see who else might want to do this business! In between posts, check for things to respond to or questions to answer throughout the comments and possibly through private messages.

Since I do not believe in using a set script, I am not going to tell you exactly what to post within your live party but I'd encourage you to think about how you can best touch on all of your offerings. Whenever possible, use an image or video but know that plain text posts work too, if you can't do that. Remember how I mentioned that simpler is better? This is especially true during the live portion of your party, as your guests will be wanting to see how this is done, and putting themselves in your shoes to see if they might be able to do this business.

Some ideas for posts during the live parties might be:

- Winner of the door prize drawing (you can do this at the end instead, too!)

- Opening talk or your "Why Story" image or video

- Posts about you or your host's favorite products

- Host Rewards and booking information

- Starter kit information or benefits of your opportunity. You might also do an "Ask me about my business" type of post or game to generate activity.

- Thank you post/reminder of how to order and when the party closes.

- Perhaps use Facebook Live to demonstrate something or even conduct an "after party" to answer any questions.

Whatever you post within the live portion of the party can also be commented on by you, your host and her guests. You can add additional information, product pictures and comments within each post to be more thorough, if you like. If you are doing a thirty-minute live party, this can get a little "fast and furious" but that is what makes it fun!

Continue to answer comments/questions after you "stop" the party, and guests will come in and out as they see posts or just want to revisit what was discussed. Tag guests in your reply comment if they asked a specific question, to make sure that they see it.

Another Option for Party Time: Since Facebook has introduced Facebook Live for real-time video broadcasting, many direct selling representatives have enjoyed conducting the thirty- to sixty-minute live portion of their parties as video broadcasts. If you choose this option, be prepared with an outline and any materials you might need in order to discuss and demonstrate the same topics you would in your posts. Allow yourself some time to interact with your guests mid-way through your broadcast and at the end to answer questions. This can be a great way to truly connect with your guests and share your enthusiasm.

Day After: Do a thank you post to all who ordered (do not mention specific purchases but you can name people) and a final reminder of when you are closing the party.

Two Days After: Post one last big thank you and an invitation to book their own party. Have your host post a comment with her thanks to her guests as well, and perhaps mention what she has earned for free.

Three or Four Days After: Post an invitation to join you on your main page to learn new tips every day.

After Orders Have Arrived: Go back and visit the events page and ask them to share about their purchases or post a picture of themselves, or post a selfie with the product in the picture.

Thank them again, congratulate your host for a job well done, and let them know you'd love some help with your business and are looking for new consultants.

Follow Up!

Follow-up after Facebook parties is so important! Take the time to reconnect with your party guests so they know you aren't just "taking their money and running!" and that you truly care about their experience.

1. Call, email or private message each guest to thank them for taking action, if they did. Or if they did not yet order, book or sign up, contact them to ask them if they want to get the rest of what they wanted by booking their own party, or ask if they've ever thought about doing what you're doing. If you can, refer back to the party posts and comments to re-call what each one was most interested in, or look for clues to what you can bring up when you communicate with them. This personalized follow-up can make a big differ-ence!

2. Once or twice a day for only two to three days following the live portion of the party, post something new to let them know you are still taking orders and bookings for however long you are keeping it open, or to let them know you are looking for a teammate, or do a Thanks post when someone has booked a party, ordered or joined. Do not overdo it, but a couple of days of posts would be fine.

3. Check your notifications regularly for any comments or questions you can address that will serve your participants and keep the conversations going. Always answer and en-courage everyone participating. If you aren't sure how to

answer a question, let them know you will find out and get back to them — then use the resources you have!

4. Check private messages on both your personal Facebook Profile and your Business Page to answer questions, close sales or arrange bookings, etc.

5. Last but not least, get out there and do your booked parties and give your next hosts the same great customer service as you did for this party!

What if You Do a Lot of Facebook Parties?

Consultants who frequently do Facebook parties might want to consider running a separate Facebook Business Page just for their parties. It is completely permissible on Facebook to have more than one Facebook Business Page. However, it is important to still comply with all of your company polices and procedures, such as identifying yourself as an Independent Consultant. The downside of doing it this way would be that your guests would not be directly connected to your main Business Page on Facebook, so you would need to make sure to mention your other page in your follow-up. I even know a consultant, Jamberry's Ruthie Smith, who came up with the idea of creating a new page for every Facebook party. Then, if her host ends up joining her team, she gets to use the page as her new Business Page when she launches her business! I think that's a great idea.

If you do a lot of Facebook parties, you may even want to temporarily un-publish your Business Page while you set up your party event and pre-load it with posts, just to minimize the possibility that non-guests will see all of the event posts while you are pre-loading. It's usually not a problem. Event posts from a Business Page are regulated by the same algorithm as the main News Feed, which means only those who Facebook thinks would be interested are shown the posts. Because of this, typically only a small portion of your Page Likes see your posts unless they are already interacting a lot with your content. So if you have a lot of active likes on your Page, from people who also happen to participate in a lot of your events, they might see your Facebook party posts even if they are not directly invited. This isn't usually a problem—the more the merrier! But if you are someone who does multiple parties a week and are concerned about it, temporarily un-publishing your Page while you pre-fill your Event can minimize the Event post visibility while you set it up.

If you choose to do this, (most of you will not need to!) go to your Page Settings (top right) and at the top, under Page Visibility, click the box to un-publish the page and then hit Save.

When you are done setting up your event, go back and uncheck it to Publish the page again. This will temporarily make your Business Page invisible to all people and all websites including your existing likes, and the search engines! For this reason I recommend doing this at an "off" time such as very early in the morning or late at night, and working quickly. Those of you who need to do this will probably get the hang of it pretty easily.

Questions About Facebook Parties

I am worried my Facebook friends will see all my activity in parties because they are public. Will they?

No. Your Business Page is not externally linked to your Personal Profile, except that you need to be logged into your Facebook account to manage it. It is a separate entity that people must "subscribe" to by liking or in the case of Events, they need to join or mark themselves as "Interested."

Everyone's News Feed is personalized to them based on who you are friends with, Groups you belong to and Pages you've liked. In addition, Facebook's News Feed Algorithm (formerly known as Edge Rank) takes all of those things you are connected to, and decides which ones to show you based on your activity on Facebook and other factors. Therefore, everyone's News Feed is completely different. Your Facebook friends will only see your party posts if all of the factors that go into the algorithm apply to each of those people.

At the time this was written, studies have shown only 2.6% of all people who like a Page are shown its posts. This amount used to be much higher, so if in the past you've held Business

Page events and most of your "likes" saw the post, be aware that the "reach" has changed drastically. So even if all of your Facebook friends have liked your Page (the only way they would ever have a chance to see your party posts) only 2.6% would see the posts from your Page, and even fewer see posts from the Event unless they were invited and joined.

Note that for this advice to work, it is important that you follow my recommendation to not "join" the event as your own personal Facebook Profile. Your Business Page will be the host, and your host will be the co-host once you add her. You will want to always comment on the party posts as your Business Page as well. One way this could possibly be untrue is if you happen to have a lot of other consultants from your company who have liked your page and "lurked" in your events by reading or even interacting with posts. In this case, those consultants may certainly see more of your Facebook party posts because by interacting with your Page they have "taught" Facebook to show them more of those types of posts. As stated in the Do Not Like Each Others' Facebook Pages chapter (page 107), I do not recommend that fellow consultants like and interact on each other's Pages, so following that guideline would eliminate this issue as well.

Compared to Business Page events, when it comes to the algorithm and low visibility, the opposite is true for posts that are generated from a Personal Profile, especially public posts you generate or interact with. Your Facebook friends are much more likely to see posts you create, like or comment on from your Personal Profile because those "stories" are not governed by the algorithm as much and posts that are set to public are especially visible from and by Personal Profiles.

Facebook assumes if you are friends, you want to see their posts, and because of the likely mutual friends and the amount of viewing and interacting, Facebook tends to show you MORE from your friends' Personal Profiles, personally joined groups and personally RSVP'd or hosted events than from Pages you've liked or Page events and activity.

In addition to this, if you are still concerned, be sure to read the section in the previous chapter about what to do when you host a lot of Facebook parties. One of the recommendations there may work for you.

If the party is public, how do we handle strangers or people the host doesn't know coming into the party and commenting or entering the drawing etc.?

The tip we shared about unchecking the Event tab setting to make sure the event does not get posted to the Timeline will help with this, and this is just a risk you take. In most cases, if your Page likes are real "fans" of your business, it would actually be beneficial if they noticed the party going on and participated, and maybe even ordered.

If the parties are really simple and customized to the host and her friends, and there aren't a lot of extras, like lots of prizes or games, someone coming from the outside (friend of a friend of a guest, for example) would feel like they were intruding and probably not participate.

If this is something that you are concerned about, you could post a note in the Event description such as "This party is for Holly Host's friends. If you don't know Holly Host, but are interested in ABC Company, please contact me!"

Having someone participate in the party who is a problem is very rare. However, if you find someone purposely attempting to sabotage the party, you can easily click the X next to their comment to hide it and then you will have the option to delete it. Then either report or ban that person from your Page. If they are truly there to stir up trouble, I would recommend taking such action.

Again, making sure you don't have other consultants interacting in your party makes a difference as well. In almost every case I've heard of where uninvited guests participated, they were other consultants playing games in hopes of winning prizes.

Speaking of prizes, why aren't there more games listed in the Facebook party training?

In my research, and in my own experience when I was in the field, I've found that playing too many games and giving away too many prizes in social media parties can be problematic for two reasons. One is that they are often complicated and time consuming for the consultant to manage. For example, some people like to do points contests, similar to ticket parties offline, where guests can earn points for taking certain actions, such as commenting on a post, sharing a picture, placing an order, etc. The consultant then is burdened with keeping track of all the people and the points, and in a Facebook party this can be difficult because of the fact that things get moved around every time someone comments and you may not see every post or comment in order to record them fairly. But what's worse is that to the guests, it is certainly obvious that it is a bit of a hassle for the consultant, and anyone who may be thinking about joining your business may think otherwise if they are worried about having to do all that work. Simpler is always better when it comes to making your job look easy, doable, and fun—and that is what leads to good team building.

Second, when guests, especially seasoned Facebook party guests, know that you will be playing several games and they can win prizes, sales go down. People start to RSVP only for the opportunity to get a free prize, not because they are genuinely interested in hearing about your products, the booking opportunity or the business. Your host may think she has a great attendance list, but in reality fewer people order. And because they tend to participate less in non-contest posts and participate more in the contest posts, the overall engagement in the party goes down.

For these reasons I recommend doing some sort of drawing that allows you to generate excitement in the beginning such as an on-time drawing, or something that gives you a mechanism for collecting the guests' contact information. Adding in an additional game for fun, or a drawing among those who order, is fine. But parties that have a game going on constantly are usually not as successful when it comes to profit for the consultant, or rewards for your host.

This Facebook party format seems too short. Won't it be difficult to build relationships in thirty to sixty minutes?

The relationship building is primary, and it is done through commenting on pre-filled posts for the few days before the party, emphasizing engagement and interaction throughout the party, and continuing conversation through follow-up posts. The Facebook party experience is much, much more than just the "live" portion that is conducted at a certain day and time. Although many direct sellers are used to and also enjoy the ten- or fourteen-day parties that were common in the past, we have found that many hosts and their guests enjoy the shorter time frame because it feels like less of a commitment and more convenient. The shorter party is just simply easier and more duplicable, too!

I've heard you can schedule your parties through third party tools. Is that recommended?

When you look at the Facebook Parties How-To chapter on page 155, it might seem a bit overwhelming to do everything in order and be there "live" for your party as well. Luckily there are some tools that do work for the Facebook Business Page Events. In the Scheduling and Automation chapter (page 73), I mention some of these tools and most will work for scheduling parties, and will even allow you to save common posts to reuse at other parties. That said, it is very important that if you do choose to use a tool, that you still need to be there "live" to interact with your host and her guests. Use the time you save to focus on the conversations by adding relevant comments on the posts you schedule to go out. For example, if you posted about a product line and someone asks if you have something in another color, if you are there live you can easily add a picture of that product in another color as a comment on the main post. This is great customer service!

I would also caution you against any activity that may trigger a problem with Facebook. Although not usually a problem with Business Pages, in contrast to personal groups or events, having scripted and repeated content can sometimes cause a challenge. Therefore, it is a good idea to vary the types of posts you include in your parties, and the verbiage you attach as captions. No one likes a "canned" party anyway, so it's best to manually set up each party, customized to your host and her guests.

I've had public events for parties before and ended up in Facebook Jail. How is this different? I've gone to using private events now to avoid this problem.

The reason people get into "Facebook Jail" (see the How to Avoid "Facebook Jail" chapter on page 99 about how to steer clear of this!) is because they are attempting to conduct business using a Personal Profile, not a Business Page. When you start a Facebook party using the regular Events app within Facebook, or using a Group, it defaults to you being the host of the event or group under your own personal name — your profile or time-line account. Since Facebook's terms do not allow people to conduct commercial activities, that could be one reason for your trouble. At the time of this publication, there is no way for a business to participate in Facebook Groups or personal events, only Personal Profiles. For this reason I recommend always going through a Business Page.

Another reason could be because you created either a Group that is set to be open or public, or an event that is public, and you are hosting these as your Personal Profile. Consequently, every interaction with the group or event generates a "story" that goes out to your Facebook friends either via the ticker on the sidebar, or within the news feed. So every post, like, and comment you make within public groups or events creates a new post for everyone to see. These often get hidden by friends, or even marked as spam or reported. Every action like that is considered "negative feedback" on your Personal Profile, and with too many of those over a certain time, you are sure to get some function on Facebook blocked. Facebook sanctions spammers, and your sales activity may alert the Facebook compliance department that you are a spammer when you post commercial activity as a Personal Profile. It is best, like I said, to avoid this completely by following my Facebook party recommendations.

Instagram Parties How-To

For those who would like to branch out to another type of party besides in-home parties or Facebook parties, or for those consultants who know their hosts and guests love Instagram, that is another option for online shows.

Set up Instagram for Success

If you are already using Instagram, you know that it is a mobile app for sharing photos. You download the Instagram app to your smart phone and open it up when you want to share a picture with your connections. There are even fun filters and editing tools built in, and it is a wonderful social media tool for sharing "window into your world" types of posts that really help build up trust and rapport with your network.

To start an account, simply visit your smart phone's App Store and download Instagram. I recommend using your real name either in the username or the "real name" section even if you want to use a fun business-related name, too. That way it's easy for your connections to find you and recognize you in their news feed. Just be sure that, if you are using your company name, you indicate you are an independent consultant in your bio, or however your company requires you to label yourself. When you are in your account, also be sure to have Push Notifications ON and set to "From Everyone" for Instagram Direct in the settings.

Set up your Profile by uploading your profile picture, and filling out your Bio—about 150 characters. Some people love formatting this in a text document or note first so line breaks and emoji can be added—have fun with it! You also get to add a website link (not included in the character limit) and this is a great place to put your personal website link.

Starting out, use the Find Friends feature to connect with your other social media friends. Then start posting pictures and enjoy! Always be sure to add a caption to the photos you share, and a few hashtags will help you get discovered by people interested in what you post about. Some popular hashtags for direct selling are #directsales #bizopp #wahm or those that are more specific to the types of products you offer. I recommend three to five hashtags so that there are just enough to get attention but not so much that they clutter your post—*hashtagify.me* is a great app to use to find popular hashtags.

When using Instagram for business, your goal is to share images that capture people's attention and encourage them to "double tap" to like the picture, or comment and maybe even tag their friends. Hashtags and emoji are abundant on Instagram and using the Explore tab (spyglass) regularly is a must to find new people and businesses to follow. When your followers like and comment on your pictures, you might just show up in the Explore tab of their friends, which is great exposure for you!

How Instagram Parties are Different

However, the one thing you should know is that there's no way to separate out party posts from your main Instagram feed! So, if you were to have parties regularly and post similar images in each one, your entire follower list would be getting all of your party posts, every time. But there's good news! Thanks to a few resourceful direct selling leaders and some research I have done on my own, there are a few ways you can create a lively party experience, similar to a Facebook party, without overwhelming yours, your host's or your guests' followers.

On Instagram you can conduct a thirty- or sixty-minute live party, with pre-party posts and post-party follow-up just like I outlined in the Facebook Parties How-To chapter (page 155), or you can choose to do a three-day party, a ten-day party, or whatever format you prefer! Since Instagram, as of right now, does not have restrictions on posting promotional posts, you will have a lot more freedom there.

Just like for Facebook parties, you will want to make sure you have the pictures you want to use saved already, except this time, since Instagram is a smart phone app, you will want to create a folder or album on your smart phone.

Another option, especially if you want to re-post something that your home office has posted on their own Instagram, is to use one of the "Repost" apps out there to simply repost something. Instagram currently does not have a native "share" function to share someone else's posts to your own account, so that's why the Repost apps come in handy. Just be sure to start the caption with your own thoughts and enthusiasm to bring the expertise back to you.

Option 1—Conduct the Party Through Instagram Direct

Instagram Direct allows you to send a group private message from within your own regular Instagram account. I feel this option will be the best one for most direct sellers because it does not require logging out of your regular Instagram or creating multiple accounts. You also do not need to be "friends" with the host or party guests in order to do this. You simply need to know their usernames.

The downside to this option is you are limited to adding only fifteen people to an Instagram Direct group message, although with good host coaching and being intentional about who is invited, your host should be able to easily get fourteen Yeses to her party. You would simply request the usernames and conduct the party with those! We have seen that online parties with about fifteen active guests do very well anyway—each person truly feels valued and the conversations seem to flow more freely when there are fewer, but more targeted guests!

To conduct this type of party, coach your host to reach out to her friends individually, especially those who she knows are active on Instagram. Since she will be limited to only fourteen people excluding herself, I recommend coaching her to tell her guests that the first fourteen to confirm as attending will be allowed in the party. Have fun with creating a sense of urgency and exclusivity when she invites her friends. And of course, if she has more than fourteen who are interested, suggest that they book their own party!

Have your host explain that there will be some great information shared via their Inboxes (found on the top right of the Home screen) over the course of however long you have decided to do your party. Let her know that once she gets a firm commitment from someone to attend the party, all she needs to do is let you know their Instagram username. Encourage her to interact on your posts within the party once you start, and share her enthusiasm just like you would for a Facebook party.

Once you have the firm list of Yeses, all you need to do is start with your Welcome post. This can be a picture or a video, although Instagram videos are limited to one minute, so be sure to prepare something short and sweet in advance! Prepare to post the picture or video just like you would a regular Instagram post, but after you've added your caption, instead of sharing it to Followers as usual, click on the word DIRECT at the top. From there you can use the search box to type in your host's username and then her guests. If at any time you need to add more people to the group message, you can click the letter "I" with a circle around it, and within the group info there is a place to add more people, up to fifteen.

When you're sure it's the way you want it, click the green Send To button at the bottom and that post will go to everyone selected and it will appear in your inbox, too. Go to your Inbox and find the message and you'll be given the option to Name this Group. Name it something like, "Holly Host's ABC Company Party" and that will make the message thread easier to find in your guests' inboxes.

Your host and her guests will get a red dot notification on their Home screen inbox that they've received a message and they can Like or Add a Comment to participate in the conversation! To start the next post, simply find that group thread in your inbox and post either a new picture or video, and then write a message as a comment that will appear underneath it. Each post will remain within this group inbox and your guests can easily scroll through them and add their own comments or questions. Note that when replying to a group message with a picture, you have the option to take a picture or choose from your photo library. However, when you post a picture, it is cropped to a square shape. It is a good idea for this reason to have your images prepared in the shape of a square so that they are not inadvertently cut off.

Something I love about using Instagram Direct is that within the comment/post thread you will see people's names and a little eye icon—that shows you who has viewed the post. This is very handy for knowing the best time to post your next item, or for following up later if you know someone has not seen a particular post.

Since there are no clickable links within Instagram posts, I recommend having at least one of your posts be something that explains how your guests can order from your site (you can say that the link is in your bio) and make sure their order is attached to their host.

Option 2—Create a Separate Party Instagram Account

For this version of Instagram parties, you would create an entirely separate party account and invite your host and her guests, then gently guide them to your main account and remove them from the party account when the party is over. For this option you would need to have a new email address to set up a new account. If you do not already have a second email, you can go set one up at Gmail or Yahoo—it does not really matter since it will not be visible and this account is not something you would be connecting to your regular email address book. The advantage of doing it this way is that you can upload images, filter them, crop them and otherwise post the same way you are used to doing in a regular Instagram account. The disadvantage of using this method is that inconvenience of needing to log out of one account to use the second one.

To start, go to the gear icon at the top right of your profile to get to your settings. Scroll to the bottom and find Add Account. Enter the new email address you created. Consider naming your account something that indicates this is your party account, such as @karensparties and then use your real name to identify you. Within the settings, toggle the setting ON for Private Account. This ensures that strangers will not follow your new account and you would need to approve each member.

When you do your host coaching, make sure your host personally invites people and when they say they are a Yes or Maybe, have her give you her guests' Instagram usernames. Coach your host to ask her guests to follow your party account themselves by giving them the username or link and let them know that you will approve them on this private account when you're ready to start the party.

You can then log into your party account by accessing it on the Settings page, set up any pre-party posts you'd like, and then when you are ready to start, approve your new followers and get the party started. Simply post within the main account and the followers will see your posts within their regular news feed mixed in with their other friends' posts. I recommend that one of your first posts shows them how to turn on notifications from your account. You can even direct message them this information so they are sure to see it. To turn on notifications, they need to go to your account page and click the three little dots on the top right of your party account profile, and then click on Turn on Post Notifications. They will then be notified of new posts as long as they have push notifications turned on in their phone settings.

Because this version of an Instagram party shows up within the guests' regular news feed on Instagram, I recommend following a similar format to that explained with Facebook parties. Set up a few pre-loaded posts that guests can see when they first visit your profile and are approved, and then a few daily posts leading up to a live party. During the live portion of the party you will post five or six main party posts, which will show up in their news feed fairly close together, depending on how many other Instagram friends they follow. Instruct your host to emphasize to her friends to have their Instagram open during the party, and either watch for posts within their feed, or visit your party profile page and refresh every so often.

Conduct your party within that account, and when you are sure it is complete and your follow-up posts are done, invite everyone to un-follow this account and to join you on your main account to keep the conversations going. Then after a few days, if someone has not yet un-followed your party account, you can always go in and block them to make them leave so that your account will be emptied before you start a new party. Once you block someone and they, by any chance, want to participate in a future party of yours, you would need to go to their account and click the three dots to Unblock them or they will not be able to access your party account. After you're sure everyone has left the party account, you might choose to go in and delete your posts except for the pre-party posts so that you can re-create the live posting schedule with your next party.

A Third Option

There is a third option for doing Instagram parties that some of you might want to do, and that is to create a separate Party Instagram account for each new party. This will act similarly to an ongoing private Facebook group. I did not mention this as one of the main options since I see it as problematic and not very duplicable. In order to do this you would need to keep creating new Instagram accounts, and Instagram requires you to use different email addresses for each one! Also, you can only have one instance of the Instagram app on your smart phone as I mentioned, with up to only five linked accounts, so it is limited and you would need to log out of each account and log in each time to check in or post. It just is not going to be practical or advisable for most people, but I did want to mention it as a third option. Perhaps someone who only does online parties once in a great while would be okay with this.

So as you can see, there are some great ways to make Instagram work as one of the options for doing online parties. This is a new party format, and I am excited to offer another option for you to build your business for those who want to try it. I'm looking forward to seeing how this works for you! Good luck!

Pinterest Parties How-To

If you would like yet another option to offer hosts in addition to in-home parties, catalog parties, Facebook or Instagram parties, and you know you or your host and her guests love using Pinterest, try this version.

Pinterest can be a powerful way to build a following and share topics of interest with both your personal friends and your business network. It is also fun for a lot of people, especially women! I consider it a "visual bookmarking" method since it is a great way to save websites and ideas you love, and share them with your friends. The way it usually works is when you find something you really love out on the Internet, you "pin it" or save it to a Pinterest board or category that you've created. The post is based on an image on the site where you found it, which makes it very visual, but since it links back to that site when you click on it, it can also be an amazing traffic generator!

You can also manually upload images, and even attach a link to them. This makes it easy to promote your images and link back to your personal website. When you pin something, your followers will see it in their feeds, too, and then they can like it, comment on it, re-pin it or share it to their own networks. Pins on Pinterest not only get shared freely, but you'll find that you keep getting likes and re-pins for months after you've posted something!

Pinterest's search is powerful and many people use Pinterest as a way to discover new things to try, places to visit, or things to buy. Since 85% of Pinterest users are women and 90% of the pins are shared by women, the most popular categories to post to and search on are things women love — home decor, crafts, fashion, recipes, travel and kids! This makes Pinterest a great place to promote many direct selling businesses.

Like the other social media sites, I recommend that you not only post about your own business, but to be sure to balance your posts with a mix of non-promotional posts along with just posting things you are interested in yourself, or that you want to save for later. Pinterest makes it easy to have one account and then create a separate business board so that you can post a variety of things into appropriate boards or categories.

For example, in the course of a week you might be researching places to go on vacation and pin destinations to a travel board, and then you can research outfits to get for your trip and pin them to your style board, and then also pin your favorite products to use while traveling, and post those to your business board. All of these things will show up in chronological order in your friends' feeds among their other friends' pins. When they look through their feed, they will notice your posts and check them out. If too many of your posts are promotional in nature, it can be a real turn-off, so try to pace yourself using the 9-1-1 Code mentioned in the What to Post? Follow the 9-1-1 Code chapter that starts on page 43).

Set Up Your Pinterest for Success

Unlike Instagram, Pinterest can be used both on the web or through a mobile app. Starting your account is easy and very similar to other social media sites—simply visit the Pinterest website or smart phone app and follow instructions to upload your profile image and complete your profile. You will be able to list a brief bio, as well as start new boards and add descriptions to them.

As with all social media sites, be sure to remember to list that you are an independent consultant whenever you mention your business, or use whichever labeling is required by your company. Once you have a basic account set up, think about other categories or boards you would like to create, on any topic you might like! One of the best features of Pinterest is the ability to categorize posts in this way, and to add a description to each board. There are not any other social media sites that I know of which allow you to do this. It makes it easy to find things again as well as for people to "subscribe" or follow certain categories of yours. If you aren't sure of the types of boards you'd like yet, you can always add them on the fly as you find things to post. I recommend installing the PinIt button to your browser, since it makes sharing items to Pinterest as you come across them much easier.

One of the easiest ways to start posting things and filling up your boards is to connect to your Facebook or Twitter friends and re-pin some of their posts. Also play with the search function and see what you can find. Pinterest even shows you trending topics, which are great. Another useful place to find content to share is with the category listing on the right of the search bar when you click the three little lines. By the way, your posts can show up here as well, based on categories you've chosen for your boards. Pinterest really makes it easy to be discovered.

Conducting Parties on Pinterest

Remember that any time you pin something, it goes out to all of your connections, so it is important to *not* use your main Pinterest boards for conducting Pinterest Parties. Not only would they be public, but due to the nature of Pinterest's feed, it really would be overwhelming to see so many posts promoting your business, whether you are doing a five-day, seven-day, ten-day or thirty-minute party. People on Pinterest really want to see new things all the time, not lots of posts about the same thing.

But luckily there is an easy way to conduct a party in private on Pinterest! It's done through a feature called Secret Boards. It is up to you and your host to decide on the length of your party and the types of content you might want to post, but refer back to the Facebook Parties How-To (page 155) and Instagram Parties How-To (page 181) chapters for some general guidelines, and be sure to tap into your company-provided images, as well as your personal website or even your company's own Pinterest or other social media accounts. The format you choose is up to you and would be similar to other online social media parties, but just conducted on Pinterest instead.

Here's How

Go to your account and click on your Profile. In the desktop version that would appear when you click on your name on the top right. In the mobile version click the person icon on the lower right. From there, click on the plus sign to Create a Board. Give your party board a name and description, such as Holly Host's ABC Party (just like you would name a Facebook party) and write in some information for your guests. Give your board a category such as Products, and then find the button that says Secret and toggle that ON. Later you are going to want to add people as Collaborators, but skip that initially and click the Create button to finish creating the secret party board.

If you like the idea of pre-filling your party with informational posts so that there is something to browse as guests arrive, you can do that before inviting people. Check back into the Facebook Parties How-To chapter (page 155) for ideas of what you can post in your party since you would be making the same type of posts — images or videos. Choose from your computer and upload to your party board, or find posts on the web to add to your party, but whichever method you use, always add your own caption when adding pins. If you are uploading images that your company has provided, or that you are allowed to use, or that you've taken yourself, you can also add in your own website link in case one of your guests clicks on the picture to go to the website. Some direct sellers like to save posting the shopping link until the end of an online party and keep it purely visual, but that is up to you.

Once you have the board the way you like it with a few informational posts or videos, you can begin inviting guests, starting with your host, of course. Coach your host to personally invite people to her Pinterest party in the same way we suggested in the Facebook Parties chapter (page 155), so that she is not adding people who do not want to be there. She needs to collect their email addresses this time, though, so that you can easily add people to the board even if you aren't Pinterest friends with them. Once she has her Yes and Maybe list together, add her to the party.

When you are ready to start your daily posts, start inviting guests. You will go into Edit Board and where it says Add Collaborators, you can add people either by username if you follow each other, or by email address. Carry on with your online party in the same way you would for other parties such as on Facebook or Instagram, posting daily perhaps and maybe with a live portion—if you've chosen that format. No one but the invited guests will have access to the board—because it is secret. All the members can stay in the group as long as you or they wish, and they can revisit the board any time. Many people like using Pinterest because it creates a group-like atmosphere where guests can stay in the board and comment any time into the future without you having to remove them.

This secret party board will appear in guests' profiles, but only to them, in their list of boards at the bottom, which is where secret boards go. I recommend doing some follow-up posts, including a post after they've received their orders. Your goal is to keep the conversation going. Make sure they know how to reach you if they want to book a party, order some more product, or become a consultant. Stay in touch with them.

Private Message Parties

There is another way to have a Pinterest Party when you are using the mobile app, and that is through a group private message, similar to how I described the Instagram Direct method of doing an Instagram party. This only really works on the mobile app because you can't pin images in the desktop version of private messages. If you like the idea of having one threaded chat conversation and working with a small group, you would conduct the party through direct message within Pinterest in the same way we talked about in the Instagram Parties How-To chapter on page 181.

To do these, you would need to have your party posts presaved into one of your boards—either a public or secret one—and add pins once you've started a group conversation. You are

limited to messaging only nine people, but as I mentioned be-fore, smaller online parties can be very effective.

Additional Online Marketing

Run a Facebook Contest!

There is so much confusion about what is and is not allowed as a contest on a Facebook Business Page. A lot of the confusion comes from the fact that many businesses—even large corporations, maybe your own corporate page—often skirt Facebook's own Page Promotion Terms (*facebook.com/page_guidelines.php*) and do not follow all of the rules, mostly out of simply not doing their homework.

These companies are then setting a poor example for others to follow, and many small businesses assume if so-and-so can do it, they can, too. In my world, it is better to know the regulations and comply with them, than to take any chances of having your contest or even your Business Page taken down or negatively sanctioned. Just because you see someone else doing it, it doesn't mean it's okay.

Following are the rules specific to running a contest, aka promotion, on Facebook. Only Business Pages are allowed to run contests:

Facebook Pages Terms

III. Page Features

E. Promotions

1. If you use Facebook to communicate or administer a promotion (ex: a contest or sweepstakes), you are responsible for the lawful operation of that promotion, including:

    a. The official rules;

    b. Offer terms and eligibility requirements (ex: age and residency restrictions); and

    c. Compliance with applicable rules and regulations governing the promotion and all prizes offered (ex: registration and obtaining necessary regulatory approvals)

2. Promotions on Facebook must include the following:

    a. A complete release of Facebook by each entrant or participant.

    b. Acknowledgement that the promotion is in no way sponsored, endorsed or administered by, or associated with, Facebook.

3. Promotions may be administered on Pages or within apps on Facebook. Personal Timelines and friend connections must not be used to administer promotions (ex: "share on your Timeline to enter" or "share on your friend's Timeline to get additional entries", and "tag your friends in this post to enter" are not permitted).

4. We will not assist you in the administration of your promotion, and you agree that if you use our service to administer your promotion, you do so at your own risk.

Facebook Page Contest Ideas

Below are some types of Facebook Page contest ideas that are 100% okay and legal to run on your Business Page, provided that you include **all of the above** (it's very important not to cut corners!):

- Post a picture in the comments! Choose a random commenter to win.

- Like this post for a chance to win!

- Answer this question in the comments for a chance to win!

- Complete this sentence for a chance to win!

- Answer this trivia question for a chance to win!

- Comment with a selfie holding our product!

- Comment with a picture of _____!

- Like this post for one entry, and comment for another entry!

- Comment up to five times to win! Each comment is one entry.

- Scavenger hunt! Find ____ on our website and comment with the answer to this question:___

- Rate the _____ on a scale of 1-10 to be entered to win!

- Do you prefer THIS or THAT? Comment with your choice!

- Which product should we put on sale next? Comment once with your favorite to enter.

- Rate our new product!

- Tell us about your _____.

- What is a product you wish we had? Comment to be entered to win!

- Like this post and comment with why you should win!

- Share a tip for our product in the comments to be entered to win!

- Caption this! Comment with your caption idea to be entered to win!

- What's your favorite quote/tip/advice about ____?

- Ask a multiple choice question—correct answers are entered to win.

- Guess how many ____.

- What did you do/watch/eat last night? Comment for an entry to win!

- What's your favorite song/vacation spot/beverage/etc.? Comment to be entered to win!

- Share a recipe! Each recipe counts as one entry to win.

- How would you use this product? Or What's a NEW way to use this product?

- Name our new product/service.

Example of Rules/Disclaimer

Be sure to customize this to your specific situation and contest. This is just an idea of how you can include everything Facebook requires. You can easily skip a few lines and include this toward the bottom of your post.

Rules/Disclaimer: This promotion is open to those 18 and older in the United States. Void where prohibited. By "Liking" (or commenting) you enter and agree that this promotion is in no way associated with, administered by, or endorsed by Facebook, and acknowledge a complete release of Facebook by your participation. Random winner will be chosen Friday at 3pm Pacific and announced on this post.

Free tools to help you choose winners:

- **Woobox Pick a Winner Free** (This one can pick multiple winners or export a list) **woobox.com/pickawinner**

- **FanPage Karma Good Luck Fairy** (Paste in the post URL and it picks a winner) **fanpagekarma.com/facebook-promotion**

- **Contest Capture** (Downloads likes/comments into a CSV from which you pick) **contestcapture.com/**

Remember to check your direct selling company's Internet marketing policies and procedures to make sure that running a contest such as these is in compliance. It may be that you can do them for a prize giveaway, but that you cannot offer a coupon or discount. You may be able to offer a small sample or product as a prize. Or perhaps the prize could be something fun like the opportunity to win "Fan of the Week" and have their photo featured on your Page. You may have to get creative, but always follow your company's P&P.

Read Facebook's Page Terms here:
facebook.com/page_guidelines.php

Promote Your Business in Online Directories

When I was a field leader, one of the best ways I found to build my team and sponsor people from all over into my party plan business was to get listed in online directories and in classifieds within discussion forums. You can do this too, even if you are just starting out.

With the advent of social media, some people think these "old school" ways are long gone, but I assure you they are not. In fact, with a simple Google search on "find a party plan business" or "direct selling business opportunities" you will see many such websites come up. These are things the average consumer out there might type into Google to find a new business opportunity or a consultant from whom to shop.

The reason these perform well in the search engines is because most of the people running the directories and forums have been doing so for years. Because Google gives extra points to older, established, yet dynamic websites with lots of fresh content and links, these sites rank high in the search engines.

These sites also tend to be keyword-rich, since every listing generates a description of the business and includes lots of words people might search for.

The opportunity for you then is to also get your individual business found in the search engines by participating in these sites. Each one is another "doorway" into your business, the way social media sites are. In most cases it is simple to participate, either for free or for a small annual or monthly fee if your company allows you to do that. Check your policies.

This will help you build your team, or get listed regionally in your own area. You might not see results right away, but you will over time, so I recommend choosing some and sticking with them for at least a few months if not a year.

Getting listed in these online directories and forums is not a make or break opportunity. However, I do think every company should have at least one listing whenever possible, whether placed by the home office or by a leader. If you do decide to list yourself as an independent consultant or leader, be sure to adhere to your company's Internet marketing policies, and always make it clear you are listing yourself as a representative, not the company.

Following is a list I've compiled of the most popular places to get listed. I have not personally worked with all of them, but I know that they do come up in the search engines, so they are probably worthwhile on some level. When you visit each site, look for the tab or link to Advertise, or Submit Your Company to find out what is involved in getting listed.

- Between Moms Home Party Opportunities: *betweenmoms.com/homeparty/*

- FindPartyPlanReps.com: *findpartyplanreps.com*

- Stay at Stay At Home Mom Home Party Sales Companies: *stay-a-stay-at-home-mom.com/home-party-sales-companies.html*

- Direct Selling Opportunities Business Directory: *directsellingopportunities.com/business_directory*

- Home Party Plan Network Directory: *homepartyplannetwork.com/homepartydirectory/*

- WAHM (Work at Home Mom) Paid Business Opportunity Ads: *wahm.com/business-opportunity.html*

- WAHM Forum Classified Ads: *wahm.com/forum/advertise-your-business-35/*

- Party Plan Companies: *partyplancompanies.com*

- The Work at Home Woman: *theworkathomewoman.com*

- Direct Sales Careers (Moms Network Directory): *directsalescareers.com/profiles.shtml*

- Find the Best Work at Home: *work-at-home.findthebest.com*

- The Best Direct Sales Companies — Home Party Companies: *thebestdirectsalescompanies.com/home-party-business-directory/*

- MLM Woman — Company Directory: *mlmwoman.com/company.htm*

- Sales Moms Network Company Search: *salesmoms.com/SearchCompany.html*

- WebMomz Home Party Directory: *webmomz.com/home_party_directory*

- Consultant Moms: *consultantmoms.com/bizopps.html*

- Direct Selling Business.com Directory: *directsellingbusiness.com/directory*

- Home Party Review: *homepartyreview.com*

- Direct Sales Aid Company Listings: *companies.directsalesaid.com*

- Find a Direct Sales Consultant: *findadsconsultant.com*

- NPros.com: *npros.com/directory.asp*

- RepSpace Business Listings: *repspace.com/businesses/browse*

- Business Among Moms Work at Home Opportunities: *businessamongmoms.com/work-at-home-business-opportunities/*

- Direct Sales Database: *directsalesdatabase.com*

- Join a Party Plan Company: *joinapartyplancompany.com*

Submit Your Product
to Product Review Blogs

Sending your product for a review on blogs is a great way to get exposure to a community of people, usually moms/families, in a short time for minimal costs – if this is something your company allows. When I was with a direct selling company, I did this regularly for our company, and to this day there are articles about the product that come up in the search engines and lead back to the company website.

Check with your home office and if they are okay with it, offer to send your product to a mom blogger who specifically offers PR product reviews. In exchange for receiving your free product (usually needs to be $50-$100 in value and can be a combination of products sent at your expense), she will write up an honest description about the product, your customer service, or anything she has experienced about your company throughout your communication. Sometimes they will even take and include their own pictures or video! This is great publicity if they have an active readership. Some, but not all, will gladly include your standard company description or mission statement, which may mention the business opportunity as well—although the focus is on the product. It is a good idea to send a catalog and other information along with the sample, so that they can do a thorough review.

The product reviewer will then post this review to their blog and share it among her social media connections. They also love it if you share with your social networks as well, since your readers may be interested in their blog, too! Showing off positive reviews also adds to your social credibility!

In addition some product reviewers will also ask for a giveaway item to offer their readers. I highly recommend you participate in these as well, if that is allowed by your company, as having a prize to win will encourage comments on the product review post. For example, if you offer a gift certificate or a duplicate product that was reviewed to a lucky winner, the reviewer can then set a prize guideline that encourages further activity with your business, such as requiring their readers to visit your personal website and come back to comment on what their favorite product is, or to like your business Facebook page or follow you on Twitter for an extra entry in the giveaway. Since all the entries for the prize giveaway happen on the product review blog post in the comments, these help the discoverability of the blog post (and your business!) in the search engines.

Find product review sites by searching "product review blog" and look for those who have a lot of comments and clearly list guidelines for submitting a product. There are some who do reviews but have very few comments, which indicates their following is low and therefore your return will be low as well!

I recommend reaching out to mom- or parenting-oriented blogs. These work great. Moms are very vocal about what they love—and they love to share their product finds with their friends! This does not mean, though, that your product needs to be a child-related product, but it should be something that is family-friendly and would appeal to the blog's readers, which are typically mothers and fathers. When choosing which products from your line to send in, keep that demographic in mind.

When you find some to contact, carefully choose two or three to submit to. If you do them all, it will be repetitive and your leads will not be unique, since many of the same people follow several of these blogs. It will also create duplicate reviews in the search results, which may be overwhelming to searchers. One or two great reviews is all you need to make an impact. The following chapter explains more about how to reach moms online.

Serving the Mom & Grandma Market Online

D id you know that mothers of children under five are TWICE as likely to be on social media than others? Would a mom or grandma be a great customer for you? Business is booming among the "mommy market" on the Internet, where mothers and grandmothers are shopping, socializing and earning money online like never before.

Having spent my early online and parenting roots as a digital mom myself — I started connecting with others online for my prior business as an isolated military mom with baby in a sling at the computer — I've not only been there and done that, but I was able to tap into this market to find new team members for my direct selling business. Whether you are a digital mom or grandma yourself, or just want to bring more moms into your business, I will share in this chapter some practical tips to help you access this thriving segment of the social media marketplace.

Things to Remember When Engaging with Moms and Grandmas

1. Focus on the relationship — **make friends first!** Have conversations. Show interest in them, find common ground and shared values.

2. Always ask yourself what the **"real life" parallel** would be. Would I do, say, or behave this way if I met this person at a playgroup or park?

3. Moms are discerning with their spending and often have a **frugal mindset,** putting their family's needs first before their own. Be sure to include benefit statements that reflect the value to their family, or offer a special or introductory rate.

4. Transactions can happen **any time of the day or night.** Some moms are online more during daytime naps. Others turn their computers on only after the kids are in bed. Working moms fit it in on breaks during the workday.

5. Time is often limited. Make things **easy to digest in small pieces.** Even when interrupted by kids' needs, pictures, short bulleted copy, short "tip of the day" type posts or emails work well.

6. Moms and grandmas are loyal to products they love and service providers who care. **Be of service, stay connected, and care** and you will create a friend — and customer — for life!

Tips, Tactics and Techniques for the Mommy Market

Leverage the search engines by including copy in your descriptive text that caters to moms and grandmas. How mom-friendly is your About page, your product description or your opportunity sales page? Speak to the benefits they or their family will receive. Look at mom blogs, parenting sites and magazines, or children's product catalogs for examples of how to appeal to parents.

Facebook Business Pages that target moms and grandmas are a good place to spend your Facebook time to increase visibility online. If you have your own Business Page, click the small gray flag under any other mom-friendly Business Page post in order to like and comment on them using the name of your business (from *your* Business Page). Use the Friend Lists or Interest Lists feature to sort pages and people in this market on your personal Facebook Profile.

You can also find those at *fb.com/bookmarks/lists* and *fb.com/bookmarks/interests*. See more about Interest lists in the chapter entitled Do Not Like Each Others' Facebook Pages that starts on page 107).

Twitter lists allow you to sort those you are following as well. Use a tool such as *twellow.com* to find people using the word "mom" or "parenting" or "sahm" (stay-at-home mom) or "wahm" (work-at-home mom) or "grandma" in their bio or tweets, and add them to a list in order to more easily sort your news feed. Find your Twitter lists in one of the tabs across your Twitter Profile page.

Twitter Parties are a great way to meet like-minded people on Twitter. One popular Twitter party is put on by Mom It Forward, an organization dedicated to educating and supporting moms. Register at *momitforward.com/gno*, where you can also find out the topic. Then, at the assigned times, follow the hashtag #gno (Girl's Night Out) using something like *tweetchat.com* or *tweetgrid.com* or *twubs.com*. Jump into the conversation and you'll find the other moms in the Twitter party will follow each other and begin interacting even outside the GNO time.

Forums, also known as Bulletin or Message Boards, Groups, or Communities, are the original form of social media and are still popular among the mommy market, along with Facebook groups. Within a forum you will find "threaded" discussions in folders. Open a folder and read the conversation threads, jumping in with your two cents where appropriate (no selling!) Have your business information in your forum bio and a link—if it is allowed—in your forum signature. People will seek you out once they trust you and see you engage with others appropriately. Some to try might be:

- *wahm.com*

- *citymommy.com*

- *ivillage.com*

- *cafemom.com*

- *grandparents.com*

Interest-specific forums or social media sites are great for those with shared interests. For example, there are forums or sites for home school moms, and there are forums for moms with a child who has special needs. There are also dance moms, soccer moms, cancer moms, custodial grandparents, and moms from specific heritages or specific religions. Do a Google search with the interest you have, and the word "forum" with it and see what you come up with.

Mommy bloggers are prolific writers and like to discuss the latest news in parenting, health and women's issues. They share what they are doing with their families, swap craft and recipe ideas, and more.

Seek out blogs at *blogsearch.google.com* and leave comments on interesting articles, and share them with your social media networks.

Media-based forums or blogs work well for both local and national exposure. If your local newspaper has a blog, or the ability to comment on news articles, seek out articles that appeal to parents and interact by leaving a comment. National parenting magazines often have companion websites, blogs, forums or Facebook pages. Interact with those, and also try *forums.parenting.com.* Children's television networks will also sometimes have parenting discussion groups. Try PBS's *pbs.org/parents.*

Pinterest is very popular among parents! The majority of people on Pinterest are women and they are looking for homemaking ideas, inspirational quotes, fashion ideas and children's activities. With Pinterest, it is important not to advertise but simply bookmark, or "pin" items you find on the web that are relevant and therefore are likely to get passed along. You can also just search within Pinterest and find items to "re-pin" as well. Once in a while a pin that leads to your own blog post or product photo is okay, but be sure to add text revealing some valuable tip, recipe or idea they can use.

In Closing . . .

Final Thoughts

I hope that while reading this book, you have discovered that I strive to educate and empower direct sellers to use social media to build more and stronger business relationships. I believe in both a high-touch and high-tech approach to accomplishing this following these core concepts that I teach in all of my trainings:

1. **Service-minded social media** marketing builds trust, loyalty, and a positive reputation.

2. "High tech" online tools can be **effectively and efficiently** leveraged to increase business owners' "high-touch" offline relationships.

3. The Internet and technology are not a replacement for traditional business methods, but are instead **components of an overall marketing plan.**

4. Social media marketing is about **connecting with people,** not collecting people.

5. Simplifying technology so it is understood and applied means that **anyone can play big** on the Internet.

I have a strong personal value around teaching, inspiring and empowering direct sellers to use the Internet to market ethically and effectively in a way that enhances their businesses, while also allowing them to stay true to their own personal values. If you are like me, you have learned in your direct selling career that the heart-to-heart connections you make in your business result in loyalty and friendships that last for years. The same is true for those you meet and interact with online. My hope is that by adjusting a few things you are doing online in your business that you will find your direct selling career richer and longer lasting, while getting better results in less time.

As you pursue your social media marketing efforts, I would love to hear from you! Visit me on any of my social media sites and let me how things are going or what questions you have. Join my Karen on Call program for affordable ongoing monthly support as well: *KarenonCall.com.* I hope to see you online, joining with me in uplifting the direct selling profession through ethical and effective social media marketing!

As I near my retirement, I decided to explore direct selling as a part-time business where I'll be the boss, pick my own hours, and make some extra money, too. Having worked full time in healthcare, never did I realize the opportunities provided in direct selling! At my first National Convention, Karen presented information on using social media to promote our personal businesses. Wow...her information was awesome! We stayed in touch, and I've been able to participate in additional training right from my home computer. The information I learned from Karen in how to develop my own business Facebook page was priceless! Thank you Karen for always being there to help!
Evelyn Ruppel, Ind. L'BRI PURE n' NATURAL Consultant
facebook.com/evelynruppelsskincare

Being computer literate back in the days of punched cards, then an advanced user with DOS and several programs as years went by, I was slow to get into Windows and even slower to try social media — shall we say resistant. Karen made it easy to confront Facebook. I attended her webinar on my 60th birthday, and immediately after, I made a Facebook page for myself and one for my business. Half an hour! Then I celebrated. :) Later I started one for a social group I belong to, and have joined other groups as well as encouraged others. I've even coached some on why their business shouldn't be the same as a personal page based on things I learned from Karen. Now I'm even looking at doing some targeted marketing through Facebook and looking into other social media.

Kat Calhoun,

Able to Learn Education Consultants & Tutors

facebook.com/AbleToLearn

Contributors

Heartfelt gratitude to my generous followers who contributed their thoughts and ideas to this publication (listed alphabetically by first name):

Arilys Palacios

Cora Belle Marburger

Deb Bixler

Donna Sickinger

Evelyn Ruppel

Heather Aichele

Heather Amy Price

Imee Birkett

Jennifer Allen

Jennifer Quisenberry

Jill Breheny

Jill Gannon

Kat Calhoun

Kimberly Bolton

Marcine Jenis

Mary Bacon

Michelle Archer

Monica Ramos

Rhoda Kindred

Ruthie Smith

Sandy Kreps

Tammy Forsythe

Terra Larsen

Tina Sanchez

Tina VanTil

Victoria Dohr

About the Author

Nothing replaces connecting with people in person or by phone, and as an experienced and active sales leader, Karen has **walked the walk** as she sold, booked, and supported a team offline, while expanding her reach and service online and through the media. She enjoys teaching others to discover exactly where, when and how to spend their precious time to establish a presence, while remaining true to their principles and personal business. Karen brings powerful messages of ethics, effectiveness and efficiency in social media and Internet marketing to direct selling and other home-based entrepreneur audiences. Her programs are high-content and filled with actionable strategies that can be implemented immediately.

For companies who want to grow their bottom line, or for distributors and leaders who want to have more of an impact, she offers dynamic programs based on years of hands-on experience. Understanding that you have a choice when it comes to learning about social media or bringing someone in to speak at your events, what makes Karen different?

- **Her experience** — As a pioneer in using technology in the industry, Karen spent twelve years in the field. She has seen and done it all both online and in a traditional in-home party business, leading a large organization. **She speaks the language of direct selling,** having taken the company to the Internet across the country and rose through the ranks from Consultant to top Director to Corporate trainer, until leaving that company to operate independently as a social media speaker, which she has been doing since 2009. If you are looking for a presenter who is not enrolled in or employed by any one direct selling company, she would love to work with you.

- **Her content** — It's simple, easy to implement and profit-producing, yet based on years of practical experience and continued study of social media and Internet marketing topics. Karen can help your representatives **cut their learning curves** through distilling just what's important to them in their situation, target demographic and product line, so that they can get down to business and get results. Her content is customized with real examples that model appropriate and effective tactics.

- **Her delivery** — Karen is fun and friendly and her enthusiasm and passion for the industry inspires people to make the most of their social media time. As someone who tends to bridge many age ranges, audiences **find her relatable** and they take her training to heart because she "gets" them and their lifestyle as a home-based business owner. People trust that Karen has their interests at heart and are therefore eager to implement what she teaches them. There's no hype, just practical content based on someone who is a lot like them.

- **Her professionalism** — As a paid professional speaker, Karen prides herself in exceeding clients' expectations through timely and positive communication, flexibility and excellence on stage and behind the scenes. She carefully works with meeting planners to deliver the very best and most powerful program that will lead to measurable change. As a Professional Member of the National Speakers Association since 2011, Karen holds herself to a **high standard of enterprise, eloquence, expertise and ethics**. She feels it is an honor to do what she does and she takes it very seriously.

- **Her presence** — Karen becomes part of your event — **approachable and accessible**. She will not simply arrive, perform, sell product and leave. She enjoys being at your event and getting to know your representatives and corporate team. She truly loves and supports all those involved the industry and it shows! This builds trust and a sense of comfort from your audience when she asks them to look at technology in new and sometimes unfamiliar ways.

- **Her impact** — Karen empowers home-based entrepreneurs to focus, to be more efficient and to get results fast, using strategies and **tactics they can immediately implement** following — or sometimes during — your event. Her emphasis is on inspiring direct sellers to truly connect with people online and then to continue relationship building in a combination of both new and traditional methods, not simply to collect people that might become customers.

Taking her own direct selling business to the very highest level of compensation in less than seven years was just the start for Karen Clark. As the Director of Consultant Development for the company, she created training programs for the entire field of representatives for five years before founding her company, My Business Presence. She has **practical experience in the field,** giving her a unique ability to convey her message authentically — **she has been there!**

As a fierce advocate for entrepreneurs and the direct selling industry, Karen has been honored with two Direct Selling Women's Alliance awards — the DSWA Spirit Award in 2008 and the DSWA Ambassador of the Year award in 2010. She is dedicated to helping all entrepreneurs and independent direct selling representatives **uplift the reputation of the industry** as they learn **smart and ethical** Internet marketing strategies.

Karen has been featured in Belinda Ellsworth's Step Into Success magazine, as well as The Home Business Connection, The Network Marketing Magazine, NSA's Speaker Magazine and Party Plan Magazine. She was also featured in Top Sellers Tell, a book highlighting successful home-based entrepreneurs. She is a co-author of the sales guidebook, Direct Selling Power, as well as a general business guidebook, Incredible Business. She is also a contributing author in Behind Her Brand: Direct Sales Edition by various direct selling experts, and Be A Network Marketing Leader by Mary Christensen. Karen lives with her husband Greg and their three children in beautiful Sonoma County, California.

Karen has offered such solid and applicable advice on how to engage authentically on social media. I find myself sharing her tips with my team regularly because her advice is relatable and specific enough that it answers the questions that they have about how to begin with their Business Page on FB when they are brand new or how to increase engagement if they have been in their business for a longer period of time. Some of the best advice Karen gives is to keep conversations natural, respond to the comments that come in quickly and act as if you are at a cocktail party and engage in your voice.

Karen's advice is always solid, easy to interpret, down to earth and relatable. Karen has a knack at breaking down the more complicated pieces of social media into chunks and action steps. She has helped me a great deal and I am always grateful for her authenticity, which shines through loud and clear on her social media platforms. In fact, I often feel I am asking a good friend for social media advice instead of a well-known expertise in the direct sales social media arena.

Jill Breheny,
Lemongrass Spa with Jill
facebook.com/LemongrassJill

Connect with Karen Clark
My Business Presence

Office Phone: 707-939-5709
Mobile Phone: 707-486-1927
Email: karen@mybusinesspresence.com
Mailing Address: PO Box 1264 Rohnert Park CA 94927
General Website: mybusinesspresence.com
Book Website: socialmediafordirectselling.com

Social Media Sites:
Facebook: facebook.com/mybusinesspresence
LinkedIn: linkedin.com/in/karenmarieclark
Twitter: twitter.com/mybizpresence
Instagram: instagram.com/karenmclark
Pinterest: pinterest.com/karenmclark
YouTube: youtube.com/mybusinesspresence

Use This Book
as a Training Tool

Social Media for Direct Selling Representatives is available in bulk discounts to companies and leaders, or for dropshipping as gifts for your team members. Please contact us for pricing.

Connections Press
PO Box 1264
Rohnert Park CA 94928

(707) 939-5709
info@connectionspress.com

Coming Soon:

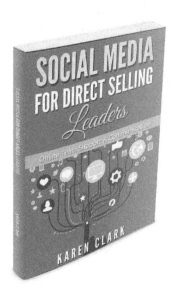

Having built her own direct selling career in the past, Karen Clark understands the responsibilities and challenges—as well as the great rewards—of being a leader in this profession. Having built a team using a combination of offline and online marketing across the United States, she knows what it is like to build and support a team long distance using technology.

In the next book in the Social Media for Direct Selling series you will learn how to:

- Establish your online presence so that you are a recruiting magnet.

- Use social media to establish your expertise as a leader.

- Develop relationships with people who say YES when offered your opportunity.

- Use technology to support and train your team near and far.

- Run a social media team group that builds a positive and success-oriented community among your team members.

- Conduct online opportunity events to help your team bring their own connections into the business.

- Use video and live streaming applications to attract and support your team members.

- Hold weekly or monthly team meetings online for training and recognition.

- Establish an annual online "virtual rally" to bring your entire organization together for a half or full day of training, inspiration and recognition online.

- . . . and more!

Are you a direct selling leader? Are you building and supporting a team or large organization? Watch for *Social Media for Direct Selling Leaders* at ***SocialMediaforDirectSelling.com***

If you would like to be one of the first to hear when this book is released, register at ***SMDSBook.com/Leaders.***

INDEX

A

Add Member, 121
Adding emoji, 115
Additional Online
Marketing, 199
Administer a promotion, 202
After party, 167
Aichele, Heather, 104
Allen, Jennifer, 81
Analytics, 68, 155
Analytics tools, 68
Avoid Common Problems,
87
Avoid Negative Comments,
93, 95
Avoiding Litigation When
Posting Images, 43, 103,
111, 158

B

Bacon, Mary, 140
Birkett, Imee, 34
Bixler, Deb, 91
Bizopp, 182, 209
Blog comments, 68
Blogs, 26, 60-61, 97, 114, 116,
211-213, 217-219
Board description, 22
Bolton, Kimberly, 86
Bonus Resources, 11
BONUS TIP, 120

Booking information, 167
Boost, 31-32, 44, 105, 122
Boosting a post, 44
Buffer App, 73
Business meeting, 43
Business Opportunity, 24,
42, 93, 115-118, 135, 156,
162, 207, 209, 212
Business Page, 21, 24, 27-33,
36-39, 43, 64, 72-75, 86, 89,
97-99, 105-109, 127, 149,
154-161, 164, 170-174,
178-179, 201-202, 217
Business Page inbox, 39
Business transactions, 149,
154
Business Values, 48, 53

C

Calhoun, Kat, 225
Category, 22, 30, 160,
191-193, 195
Chamber of Commerce, 24
Checkboxes, 160
CinchShare, 73
Clark, Karen, 1-10, 16, 20-51,
58-68, 72, 76-80, 84, 86, 90,
94, 98-130, 134-170,
174-178, 182-188, 192-196,
202-204, 208-212, 216-218,
224
Code, 9-1-1, 41, 44-45, 59, 99,

118, 192
Competitor saboteurs, 102
Conducting Parties on
    Pinterest, 194
Connected account, 26
Connecting, 1, 3, 10, 28, 58,
    75, 78, 83, 100-101, 186,
    215, 223
Contact base, 136
Contest Capture, 205
Contest posts, 177
Convention pictures, 23
Copyright infringement, 111
CORE values, 53, 59
Cover Image, 159
Create Event, 159
Customer Service, 79, 81, 94,
    170, 178, 211

D

Direct sales, 8, 10, 133, 135,
    157, 209-210
Direct selling, 1-10, 16-27,
    31-33, 37-39, 43-45, 49-51,
    55, 59-65, 69, 73, 77-81,
    85-86, 91-95, 99-109,
    113-120, 123-129, 133-145,
    148-171, 175-179, 182-189,
    192-197, 203-219, 224-225
Direct selling companies, 3,
    16, 135
Direct selling
    representatives, 3-9, 17,
    21-27, 31-51, 55, 59-65, 69,
    73, 77, 81, 85, 91, 95,
    99-109, 113, 117-129,
    135-151, 155-171, 183-197,

203-209, 213, 217-219, 225
Dohr, Victoria, 17
Door prize drawing, 165, 167
Door-to-door selling, 8
During severe weather, 138

E

Eligibility requirements, 202
Email newsletter, 68, 76, 137
Email newsletter
    subscriptions, 68
Emoji, 115, 164, 182
Engaging with Moms, 216
Event description, 159, 175
Event Name, 159
Event page, 150, 160-164, 166
Events, 9, 32, 34, 61, 73, 76,
    95, 128, 133, 140, 148-149,
    153-155, 158-159, 163, 168,
    171, 173-175, 178-179
Events tab, 159, 163
Example of Rules, 204

F

Facebook, 6, 11, 16, 19-21,
    24, 27-40, 44-46, 49-50, 55,
    64-75, 78, 84-86, 89, 95-110,
    114, 117-123, 127-130,
    133-136, 140-142, 147-184,
    187-188, 191-196, 201-205,
    212, 217-219, 224-225
Facebook account, 30, 97-98,
    110, 173
Facebook event, 32, 128, 140,
    149, 155, 158, 161
Facebook fans, 68
Facebook Friday, 99

Facebook games, 127

Facebook groups, 33-34, 73, 95, 97, 99, 121, 154, 179, 218

Facebook Jail, 73, 97, 101, 129, 148-149, 151, 153, 156, 178-179

Facebook Page contest ideas, 202

Facebook Pages Terms, 202

Facebook Parties, 133, 147-150, 153-154, 156-158, 160, 169-170, 173, 175, 178, 181, 183, 187, 194-195

Facebook Parties How-To, 153, 178, 183, 194-195

Facebook's News Feed Algorithm, 73, 149, 173

Facebook's Terms of Service, 98

Fan of the Week, 205

FanPage Karma Good Luck Fairy, 205

Final Thoughts, 223

Five core personal values, 48

Florida, 1-2

Follow-up, 32, 77, 81, 119, 138, 143, 145, 157, 161, 169-170, 177, 183, 188, 196

Forsythe, Tammy, 40

Forums, 2, 153, 207-208, 218-219

Free tools, 204

Freebie, 117

Frugal mindset, 216

Fun Friday post, 45

G

Game, 75, 120, 127, 147, 167, 175-177

Gannon, Jill, 120

General introduction, 165

Girls Night Out, 26

Giveaway, 205, 212

Gmail, 186

GNO time, 217

Golden rule, 84, 122

Google, 32, 86, 91, 94, 103, 117, 165, 207, 218

Google Forms, 32, 117, 165

Google search, 91, 207, 218

Grandma Market Online, 215

Green flags, 39, 118

Groups, 2, 25-26, 33-34, 36, 55, 62, 73, 78, 94-95, 97-99, 101, 116-117, 121, 126, 138, 140, 148-149, 154, 173, 175, 178-179, 218-219, 225

Guidelines, 10, 27, 30, 45, 120, 147, 149, 151-152, 156, 194, 212

Guidelines for Facebook Parties, 147

H

Hang out, 49, 93, 106

Happy hour, 25

Harmon, Jennifer, 153

Hashtags, 20, 23-24, 117, 182

High tech, 1, 223

High touch, 1

Holding social media parties, 142

Home shows, 138

Home-based business, 24, 44, 81, 90, 116
HootSuite, 73
Host Coaching, 141-142, 163, 184, 187
Host Rewards, 135, 137-138, 146, 162, 167
How to Add Pages, 108
How to Use This Book, 7
How-to, 11, 21-22, 42, 60, 149, 152-153, 162, 178, 181, 183, 191, 194-196
How-To chapter, 178, 183, 195-196
Humanity in marketing, 58

I

Ideas to Try, 22-23, 25-26, 28, 36, 38-39
Incentive trip pictures, 23
Increase your exposure, 21, 24
Independent representative, 7
Informational posts, 156, 161-162, 195
Inspire people, 64-65
Instagram, 5, 20-21, 23-24, 31, 36-37, 46, 49, 68, 73, 75, 95, 117-118, 127, 141, 181-189, 191, 193-194, 196
Instagram Direct, 182-185, 196
Instagram Parties, 181-182, 186, 188, 191, 194, 196
Instagram username, 184, 187

Interest List, 31, 98, 108, 217
Interest-specific forums, 218
Invite button, 144, 163-164

J

Jenis, Marcine, 69

K

KarenonCall.com, 5, 224
Keyword-rich, 208
Kindred, Rhoda, 39
Kreps, Sandy, 78

L

LinkedIn, 19-21, 24-25, 35-37, 68, 73, 86, 117, 127
Long distance friends, 138

M

Mail a postcard, 144, 150
Marburger, Cora Belle, 114
Marketing plan, 223
Media-based forums, 219
Mobile app, 181, 193, 196
Modeling for others, 16
Mommy market, 215-216, 218
More About Facebook, 29
Multi-tiered pay plan, 7
My Story, 1

N

National Speakers Association, 231
Negative feedback, 179

Network Marketing
representatives, 8-9
Network Marketing/MLM,
8-9
News Feed, 29, 36-37, 73, 75,
108-109, 122, 127, 149, 171,
173, 179, 181, 187, 217
Non-competing pages, 117
Non-contest posts, 177
Non-marketing messages, 42
Non-quality Likes, 109-110
Not Collecting, 1, 10, 76, 83,
100, 223
Note About Polyvore, 112

O

Online Directories, 207-208
Online parties, 8, 49,
133-138, 140, 144-145, 148,
153, 156-157, 184, 189, 197
Opening talk, 158, 167
Organic Social Media, 75

P

Page Features, 202
Palacios, Arilys, 66
Parenting-oriented blogs, 212
Party Plan, 8-9, 207, 209-210
Party Plan representatives,
8-9
People Before Things, 83-84,
86
Person-to-person sales, 8
Personal persona, 48
Personal profile, 21, 24-25,
27-30, 32-33, 36-37, 98, 100,
144, 149, 154-155, 161,

173-175, 179
Personal Timeline, 97-100,
102, 108, 202
Pin business, 23
PinIt button, 193
Pinterest, 20-22, 31, 36-37,
49-50, 68, 73, 81, 90-91,
141, 191-196, 219
Pinterest Parties, 191, 194
Pinterest's feed, 194
Pixabay, 43
Polyvore's terms, 113
PostCron, 73
Pre-filling, 162, 195
Pre-loaded posts, 187
Pre-loading, 170
Pre-party posts, 161, 183,
187-188
Pre-populate the event, 150
Price, Heather, 55
Private Facebook group, 20,
95, 188
Private message, 26, 30, 39,
64, 80, 95, 97, 101, 118-119,
125, 143, 148, 150, 166,
169-170, 183, 196
Private Message Parties, 196
Professional networking
event, 24
Promote Your Business, 41,
100, 123, 207
Promotional posts, 42, 119,
183, 192
Promotions, 202
Public domain, 111
Publish Events to Timeline,
159

Q

Questions, 4-5, 25, 33-34,
42-43, 48-49, 57, 59, 63-64,
76, 80, 84-85, 107, 136, 157,
164, 166-170, 173, 185, 224
Quisenberry, Jennifer H., 51

R

Ramos, Monica, 110
Reach moms online, 213
Real name, 30, 98, 181, 186
Reasons to Do Online Social
Media Parties, 137
Reply, 26, 36, 38-39, 72, 77,
80, 84, 101, 168
Repost apps, 183
Resource Page, 4, 11, 21, 102,
114
Return on Interaction, 67
Return on Investment (ROI),
67
Reverse image search, 103
Review Blogs, 211
Roll call, 165
Rules, 16, 29, 98-99, 101-102,
104, 111, 120, 149, 154,
201-202, 204
Rules/Disclaimer, 204
Running a contest, 201, 205
Ruppel, Evelyn, 224

S

Sanchez, Tina, 46
Scavenger hunt, 203
Scheduling and Automation,
38, 71, 178

Scheduling posts, 71
Search engines, 25, 31, 37,
57, 64, 76, 86, 171, 207-208,
211-212, 216
Secret board, 22, 194, 196
Secret Team Support Board,
23
SEO-oriented keyword
searches, 76
Serving your customers
online, 80
Setting Up Your Business
Page Event, 158
Settings, 8, 15, 30, 98, 101,
125-126, 159, 171, 182,
186-187
Share a post, 22
Sickinger, Donna, 28
Snapshots, 23
Social Media Best Practices,
13
Social Media CPR, 35, 39, 80
Social Media Do's and
Don'ts, 121, 155
Social media marketing, 5,
10, 16, 20, 48, 53, 57-58, 67,
94, 223-224
Social Media Parties, 9, 33,
131, 133-135, 137, 139-142,
148, 153, 163, 176, 194
Social Media Parties Pros &
Cons, 133, 148, 153
Social media platforms, 11,
50, 66, 76, 121
Social Media Post Ideas, 37,
57
Social media sites, 19-21, 24,
26, 30, 33, 35, 37-38, 42, 44,

73, 75, 89, 127, 192-193, 208, 218, 224
Social Media Voice, 47
Spammer, 179
Staying in compliance, 10
Suggest Page feature, 31

T

Tags, 36, 160
Tech support, 5
Techniques for the Mommy Market, 216
TinyTorch, 73
Transparency, 84
Trivia question, 203
Turn on Post Notifications, 187
Tweet chat, 26
Twitter, 5, 17, 20-21, 24-26, 35-37, 49-51, 68, 73, 75, 84, 117-118, 122, 127, 193, 212, 217
Twitter followers, 68
Twitter lists, 217
Twitter party, 26, 217
Twitter Profile page, 217

U

Un-publish, 170-171
Using Questions for Post Ideas, 63
Using social media, 4, 15, 34, 48, 58, 64-65, 224

V

VanTil, Tina, 130
Visual bookmarking, 191

W

Wahm, 182, 209, 217-218
Washington, 1-2
Ways to attract the right people, 115
Website link, 30, 43, 99, 160, 182, 195
Window into your world, 23, 89, 181
Women business, 43
Woobox, 204
Word Dream, 24

CPSIA information can be obtained
at www.ICGtesting.com
Printed in the USA
BVHW061604010419
544233BV00026B/2514/P